The Cost of a Best Seller

BY FRANCES PARKINSON KEYES

Fiction

JOY STREET
DINNER AT ANTOINE'S
CAME A CAVALIER
THE RIVER ROAD
ALSO THE HILLS
CRESCENT CARNIVAL
ALL THAT GLITTERS
FIELDING'S FOLLY
THE GREAT TRADITION
PARTS UNKNOWN
HONOR BRIGHT
THE SAFE BRIDGE
SENATOR MARLOWE'S DAUGHTER
LADY BLANCHE FARM
QUEEN ANNE'S LACE
THE CAREER OF DAVID NOBLE
THE OLD GRAY HOMESTEAD

Non-Fiction

THERESE: SAINT OF A LITTLE WAY
THE GRACE OF GUADALUPE
THE SUBLIME SHEPHERDESS
ALONG A LITTLE WAY
CAPITAL KALEIDOSCOPE
SILVER SEAS AND GOLDEN CITIES
LETTERS FROM A SENATOR'S WIFE

Poetry

THE HAPPY WANDERER

Juvenile

ONCE ON ESPLANADE

The Cost of a Best Seller

BY

FRANCES PARKINSON KEYES (wheeler) 1885-

Illustrated by Susanne Suba

5 3- 32281

JULIAN MESSNER, INC. NEW YORK

PUBLISHED BY JULIAN MESSNER, INC.
8 West 40th Street, New York 18

PUBLISHED SIMULTANEOUSLY IN CANADA BY
THE COPP CLARK COMPANY, LTD.

COPYRIGHT 1950 BY FRANCES PARKINSON KEYES
PRINTED IN THE UNITED STATES OF AMERICA

To Deanie

WHO DOES NOT SPARE HER COMMENTS

SHE QUESTIONS MY SPELLING

and

CORRECTS MY SLANG

and

TELLS ME MY HERO'S TYPE OF LOVE-MAKING

WENT OUT WITH HOOP SKIRTS

BUT STILL SHE SEES RED WHEN

ANYONE ELSE CRITICIZES UNJUSTLY

and

WHAT IS MORE,

NO ONE, EXCEPT MYSELF, KNOWS BETTER

THAN SHE DOES

The Cost of a Best Seller

BUT STILL SHE STANDS BY

The Cost of a Best Seller

Ever since I can remember I have wanted to be a writer. As a matter of fact, at the age of seven, with collaboration from a contemporary, I wrote the script for a pageant in twelve scenes, which as many excited little girls, myself among them, produced in my mother's drawing room on Beacon Street. The manuscript was preserved by my collaborator, and triumphantly displayed by her to an astonished group, during the vogue of *The Young*

Visiters, in refutation of the charge that a child as young as Daisy Ashford could not possibly have created the inimitable Mr. Salteena, not to mention various other characters in the same story. "I should like to know why not," my friend said in a challenging manner. "Just look what Frances and I wrote, our first year at Miss Carroll's!"

I do not think she persuaded anyone that our efforts were comparable to Daisy Ashford's achievement; but there was no denying that the script, while almost wholly lacking in punctuation, and carrying simplified spelling to very great lengths, did have form and substance. I had entirely forgotten its existence when my friend unearthed it, and I must say that its discovery and reception gave me great encouragement; for those were the days when most of my acquaintances could easily have been placed in two categories: the outspoken ones who said brutally, "You're working on a novel? Well, I hope you don't expect me to buy it!" and the more merciful ones who murmured, "Listen, I'll be glad to buy your book when it comes out. That'll make one copy sold anyway."

These remarks were almost equally crushing in their effect; therefore I was in a mood to welcome anything which would raise my spirits and bolster my morale. For though I had begun to write at so tender an age and had gone doggedly on doing so, I did not have much to show for this by the time I was thirty. My mother had been pleased with the pageant, and she was also favorably impressed with some verse of fervently patriotic nature, which I wrote during the Spanish-American War and which was published in the small weekly newspaper of the Vermont township where our ancestral home is located. But after that she lost interest, and eventually she lost her temper, when a romantic offering, whose dispatch I had not mentioned, was returned to me by the *Boston Transcript*. (I had sent no stamps with it and had fondly believed it would be buried in oblivion if it were not acceptable. I am still puzzled because this did not happen.) She read the verses with disapproval, and sternly forbade me to write any more, saying she would pack me off to boarding school if I did. As I had no desire to go to boarding school, I took no further chances of getting caught; but I went on writing just the same, hiding the products of my pencil in a deep drawer, under my Ferris waists.

When I married, at an early age, I found that my husband was no more disposed to regard my literary efforts with a favorable eye than my mother had been. By that time I was used to writing in secret, however, and I went on doing so. A New England attic provides an excellent retreat from prying eyes, and there are always a few minutes every day when the children are asleep and when no household task requires immediate attention—or at least it was so in my case. But I had grown extremely sensitive on the subject of my writing; if neither my mother nor my husband believed in it, how could I reasonably expect that anyone else would do so? The conviction that I could not became so strong that I doubt if the ruled copybooks, filled with penciled scribblings, of which there were eventually quite a number, would ever have seen the light of day, if the family fortunes had not been at such low ebb that it was evident more money must come from somewhere. I was ill a great deal, I had three young children and I did not see how I could dispense altogether with domestic service; I had never been trained to a profession or indeed to anything useful; but I was eager and determined to help my husband in some way if I possibly could. Desperately, because I could think of nothing else to do, I drew one of the ruled copybooks from its hiding place. Then, with the assistance of a resourceful hired man, I restored a battered and monumental typewriter that had been relegated to the same attic which was my own retreat. I think this typewriter must have represented Mr. Remington's first inspiration; but on its noisy double keyboard I ineptly copied one of my penciled stories, stealing fifteen minutes a day for the work. When it was finished, I awaited my next trip to Boston and myself carried the typescript to a publisher,

4

whom I had previously summoned up courage to consult as to the best method of submitting a novel. He had regarded me with amusement and had told me not to tie up the script with a pink ribbon. I do not think he ever expected to see me or hear from me again. However, he received me mercifully when I reappeared, and promised that if the script were not acceptable, he would respect my request that it should be returned to me in care of a sympathetic friend and not to my home address. I was taking no chances of a repetition of the *Transcript* episode.

The script was not returned and, though the novel based upon it received neither a startling sale nor rave reviews, it furnished the wherewithal to pay all outstanding doctors' bills and to provide me with a new spring outfit, the first I had had in a long while. It did far more than that. It restored my faith in myself as a human being—and as a writer. I recognized that it was the first landmark in a career which I was justified in pursuing without shyness and without shame. I plunged ahead, stumbling as I went, but still forging haltingly forward on my chosen road. It was by no means easy going and I did not get rapid results from the work which I continued to do in the same plodding way as before, though I no longer hid as I wrote. Each novel sold a few more copies than its predecessor, but that was not saying much. Articles, for a long time, did better;

therefore, though I had started out as a novelist and hoped that I could someday return to the field of fiction, I spent most of my time and strength on articles; they brought in more money than fiction and my contribution to the family budget was of prime importance. I was sent into many parts of the world to write them and they met with a very generous response. Some of them were gathered together in book form and also did moderately well. Eventually I was asked to write the biography of a saint and, with many misgivings, I undertook this. While working on it, I was able to write, for the first time, in an atmosphere of great peace, among surroundings of complete tranquillity. After a long period of strain and stress, this quietude, from the beginning, was like a healing pool and, in due course, it became a wellspring of inspiration. The following fall, seventeen years after the appearance of my first novel, I produced my first best seller.

II

Honor Bright, the heroine of this book, was presented as a writer and I caused her to say, in speaking to her publisher of a book she had written: "It's like this . . . naturally I hope this . . . story . . . will have a huge success. Naturally I'd like to see it a big serial and a best seller and a million-dollar movie. Any writer would like that. Any writer would be pleased and proud to have something like that happen. But even that, important as it would be, would be merely incidental. What really counts is that I've put everything I have and everything I am into this story— all the study, all the thought, all the workmanship, all the effort, of which I am capable. There isn't a line in it that's slipshod or superficial or insincere. There's nothing repressed which represents a vital truth, because the revelation of it might prove startling or shocking. On the other hand, there's nothing told simply because it would cause a sensation, because it's permeated with pruriency and grossness. That's the way I feel writing ought to be—flowing and free and beautiful. That's what I want *my* writing to be. That's what I've tried to make it. I may have failed, but I've tried. And that's what really counts."

Though I did not realize it at the time, afterward I recognized that, in this passage, I was unconsciously quoting my own creed. When the limp yellow letter came in, announcing the acceptance of my first novel, I had sat for a long while with it in my hands, reading and rereading it; and as I did so I had made a vow: that I would never let any work leave my hands which was not as good as I knew how to make it—not as good as I hoped it might be someday, not as good as another writer could turn out, but the very best of which I was capable at the moment. I had promised myself that no matter how much I needed money, I would not write hastily or casually; that I would do my utmost to improve my craftsmanship; that I would give every subject on which I wrote careful thought and careful study; and that I would begin and end every working day with prayer. I knew from the beginning that writing is not just a trade, but a trust, and that an author who is unworthy of such a trust is betraying it, in the same sense as an architect who erects a structure without due regard for its safety or a physician who breaks the Hippocratic oath.

To the best of my ability, I had kept my vow and been faithful to my creed over that long stretch of years between the appearance of my first novel and that of my first best seller. But for many reasons, those years had been hard ones. The physical strain had been very great. I had never failed to fulfill an assignment, but I had six times gone aboard ship on a stretcher, because I was too ill or too crippled to do so otherwise. I had fainted away, from exhaustion or pain, at more than one press table. A bad fall, occurring early in the course of a trip around the world, resulted—largely through the unavailability of proper diagnosis and care for more than a year—in a spinal ailment so serious that I was condemned to wear a steel harness for the rest of my life. I had been through numerous hurricanes and earthquakes, two or three epidemics and several revolutions. For extended periods of time I had been away from my home, of which I am extremely fond, and for other extended periods I had seen almost nothing of my friends because the length of my working hours precluded me from enjoying their company. Moreover, because of my long absences, it had been necessary that my housekeeping should be doubly intensive when I was at home, and this also consumed a great deal of time and strength. People began to refer to me as "indefatigable" and I resented this, because I was exhausted most of the time; but since I never had a vacation, I never had a chance to recover from this exhaustion and I knew I never would, as long as I went on working so hard to make both ends meet. To be sure, as I became more successful, I had not lacked for opportunities to take things more easily; but these opportunities had been in the form of remunerative offers for work which was not in accordance with the standards of any conscientious writer and even for "the use of my name" attached to work which I had not done at all. Their acceptance was unthinkable.

That first novel of mine which appeared on a best seller list did not mount very high or remain there very long. But, as I gazed at its title, coupled with my name, on that fascinating chart, I told myself triumphantly that my troubles as a writer were over—well, very nearly over. Of course the next novel would do better still, and the next one better than that, and so on. Presently I would be earning enough money so that I would not have to work unless I felt equal to it, physically and mentally, or under any other conditions which were not pleasing to me. I was through with writing on river steamers where a board placed across a washbasin served as a desk and in small primitive inns where there was no heat and where one feeble electric bulb in the ceiling supplied the only light. I was through with separations from my nearest and dearest. Henceforth I would write at home, in the bosom of my family, surrounded by every comfort, and I was going to take time to enjoy this. For I was also through with working twelve hours a day, seven days in the week and fifty-two weeks in the year. It had taken me seventeen years to reach the point where I could say this, but that point had now been attained. I said it and I meant it. I thought I was justified in doing so.

I could not possibly have been more mistaken. I still had to learn that Ernie Pyle was right when he said, "There is no easy way to do your work. . . . However it may seem to you, writing is an exhausting and tearing thing."

III

My first mistake was in visualizing the financial returns from a best seller in terms of advance royalties which would mount in size with each successive book, if its predecessor had done well, and of sales which would become correspondingly greater. I realized, of course, in a general way, that the more money I had, the more Uncle Sam would exact from me in taxes—and this irrespective of the fact that it was earned and not inherited money and of the further fact that my tardy arrival in the high-income bracket meant that nearly twenty years of adult life had gone into learning my craft and that this period of no-vitiate represented investment but no profit. What I did not realize was that, in order to get the large advance royalties and the vastly increased sales, I would have to spend a corresponding amount of money myself!

I could give a great many examples of this, but I think one or two will suffice: my novel, entitled *The River Road*, brought me in a good deal of money—on paper; but in order to make it authentic and convincing, I myself had to go and live on the special stretch of River Road which I was attempting to interpret. (I have long made it a practice to settle in any region that I use for a setting. On this occasion, however, there was not merely a question of personal practice; there was a question of professional requirement.) The only available house was one of great beauty and historical significance; but it had not been occupied for many years and it was in a sad state of disrepair. Moreover, it had never been equipped with many modern conveniences —not even a kitchen sink. Its owners agreed to lease it to me if I would put it in good condition, and I accepted their terms because there was literally nothing else I could do if I were to write the book for which I was under contract.

By the time I had equipped this twenty-room house—inexplicably called The Cottage!—with the minimum amount of plumbing requisite for decent living, with enough gas heaters to insure a reasonable amount of warmth and

14

enough lighting fixtures to read and write by, I had spent really staggering sums and these represented only the beginning of my outlay. The house had to be painted throughout; it had to have clothes closets, pantry shelves and a linoleum-covered, board floor in the kitchen. (There had been only a rough brick pavement there before.) And none of these essentials was easy to come by. Daily, as I besought the services of a workman or went shopping for a roll of wire, I was asked if I did not know there was a war on. (I did know it all too well; I had a dearly loved son overseas.) When I look back on the months that I spent in making that house habitable—months, needless to say, when I accomplished very little writing—they seem to me among the most trying I have ever spent in connection with my work.

When I was finally settled in The Cottage there were further complications: I had neither mail nor telephone service; anyone who has ever tried to conduct a big business without them—and by then my writing constituted a big business—will have some idea what this meant in the way of a handicap. I had no delivery of any commodity; every morsel of food eaten in that house, every drop of water drunk, was brought out from town, eight miles away. The Rationing Board was understanding and considerate; in addition to some coupons for use in case they were needed during the process of securing source material, I was given a gasoline allowance sufficent for one daily trip to town. My secretary brought food, water and ice out with her in the morning and took a list away with her when she left at night; but if anything was forgotten in the way of provender, we went without, if there was unexpected company, portions were smaller. After my secretary had left in the evening, my housekeeper, Clara Wilson, and I were entirely shut off from the world, unless we had guests. The spinal difficulty to which I have previously referred has always prevented me from driving a car; if either Clara or I had been ill in the night there would have been nothing to do about it; we had no way of calling a doctor or sending anybody to fetch one. Neither could we have summoned help if there had been a robbery or a fire. I am not a timid soul, but I could not help thinking of all these things, when I had a sudden, inexplicable pain or when mysterious noises sounded through the gloom.

In saying that I am not a timid soul, I should perhaps qualify the statement. Under normal circumstances, I enjoy being alone in a house; it gives me a welcome sense of detachment and peace. As a girl, I rode horseback every day that I was at our country place in Vermont; and it was immaterial to me whether I did so astride or sidesaddle or with no saddle at all. This experience stood me in good stead when I began riding in the Yosemite Valley, long before the days when automobiles were allowed there, as almost any kind of mount had to "do." Later on, in Germany, I went in for jumping and the higher the hurdles, the better I liked them. Only the spinal condition, to which I have previously referred, put an end to my riding. No horse ever could have done it. I swam with the same sense of untroubled security; and I have no dread of possible accidents when I step into an airplane or an automobile; in fact, as far as the latter is concerned, I have often been accused of being a "speed demon" and speedboating or, for that matter, any kind of boating, is one of my favorite diversions. I went through the various hurricanes, earthquakes, epidemics and revolutions aforementioned without the slightest feeling of fear and, indeed, without losing a night's sleep or missing a meal. I have no recollection of any terrified sensations in connection with my voyage on the *San Pedro*, the small French freighter on which I returned from Europe six weeks after the outbreak of World War II—and this in spite of the fact that the sea was strewn with submarines, and that I wrote my biography of St. Bernadette while wearing a life preserver, and keeping within easy reach a small bag containing the essentials which I might require in a lifeboat. Moreover, all kinds of wild animals leave me quite unmoved; so do spiders, mice, rats and roaches. But I have a horror of snakes which entirely transcends fear.

I am not afraid of what they may do to me; a snake bite is far less likely to be fatal than an automobile accident and is probably far less painful; but the sight of them, either alive or dead, and even the awareness of their presence, actual or probable, affects me in a way that no one who is not afflicted with the same phobia can possibly understand. And Louisiana is, all too literally, a paradise infested with serpents. According to a standard work of reference, the state "has forty different species of snakes, six of which are poisonous and represent a definite hazard to all who work or play outdoors." *

The knowledge of this made me hesitate for a long time before deciding to make Louisiana my writing center during the winter months; I knew how much suffering on that special score was ahead of me—or rather, I thought I did. More than once I had read articles in New Orleans papers about homecomers who had been obliged to beat a hasty retreat into their bus because a rattlesnake was coiled at their scheduled stop—well within the city limits; and in the contributors' columns of those same papers appeared letters from worried householders who lived near vacant

* Robson, John B., *Louisiana's Natural Resources: Their Use and Conservation* (New York: Silver Burdett & Company).

lots where the denizens of uncut grass constituted a source of danger to their children. Friends of mine residing in smaller cities had told me even more lurid tales; but even the most upsetting of these accounts had not prepared me for the prevalence of snakes around The Cottage.

I tried to make it a practice, when I first went there, to wedge in a short walk between working hours and supper; I gave it up, not only because it became increasingly difficult to find the time for it, but because snakes so frequently slithered across my path or writhed in the road ahead of me that I could not dismiss from my mind the dread that one would do so, even when I did not see any. But even the abandonment of my walks—the only form of exercise left to me—did not free me from the cause of my shrinking apprehension. One evening when I opened the door leading from the entrance hall to the rear patio, to let out my cocker, Lucky, for her nightly airing, I saw—just in time—that a snake lay dormant across the step. Shortly thereafter, I loaned The Cottage to a bridal couple of whom I was very fond; one night, as they were undressing, they became aware of something stirring under their bed. It proved to be a snake. After that, when I heard noises in the night, it was hard to convince myself that they could be caused by anything else. With all the will power that I was able to summon, I tried to overcome this phobia; as I grew more and more tense from overwork, lack of exercise and loss of sleep, the harder this became.

The book which I had agreed to write required a great deal of research and a great deal of expert advice. Its story concerned the rising and falling fortunes, over a twenty-five-year period, of a family living on a sugar plantation, located beside the Mississippi River. When I started the novel, I knew next to nothing about the cultivation of sugar. I visited more than a score of sugar mills, read more than forty books and consulted well over a hundred persons before I was sure of my background material. This had to be drafted with meticulous care, after consultation with competent authorities, and then read back to these persons, to be sure it contained no factual mistakes. Afterward, it had to be redrafted, in more finished form. The flood conditions to which the region is subject constituted another unfamiliar angle; so did the various types of hunting and other sports prevalent in the locality; a corresponding amount of time and care went into the interpretation of these. Numerous colloquialisms and dialects, not in current use farther north, are indigenous to the vicinity; a failure to reproduce these correctly would have lessened the illusion of reality in the book. Whenever I talked with a new acquaintance, either white or black, I listened carefully for peculiarities of speech and, as soon as I was alone, I jotted these down. After I had incorporated them in my text, I consulted another acquaintance as to whether I had done so accurately and effectively.

When I had been working on the book about six months I was taken ill, and my physician advised me to limit myself to three working hours a day. I was already far behind my schedule, because of many unavoidable delays, and this lateness represented a serious loss, not only to myself but to my publisher. The average lay person seems quite oblivious of the fact that a publisher maps out his program long before a book's appearance in print: salesmen are sent all over the country to take advance orders for it; an advertising campaign is inaugurated; if there is a paper shortage—as there was throughout the war—available amounts are carefully allocated. If a publisher has counted on a book for fall publication and then fails to receive it, he stands to lose thousands of dollars. No conscientious author will allow his publisher to undergo such a loss, if he can possibly help it, still less will he involve his publisher in losses for two successive seasons. When my physician told me to curtail my writing hours, I replied that I simply could not do it. He shrugged his shoulders and said that, under those circumstances, he would not be responsible for the consequences.

The months dragged along. I was terribly troubled

about having failed my publisher and terribly worried about my own finances. The advance royalties on my next book would, of course, not be due until *The River Road* was finished, nor would my publisher be in a position to pay them until he had realized a profit on that. But I had not counted on being without supplementary funds for so long or on the expense of maintaining such a costly establishment as The Cottage indefinitely. I borrowed money on all my securities and, realizing that I could not borrow more, every morning I forced myself to get out of my bed and go to my desk. Some days when an open copybook was actually in front of me and a pencil actually in my hand, the words began to come almost of themselves, and by night I had covered from fifteen to thirty pages with my scribblings. Other days I managed to cover only a few pages, a sentence or even a word at a time. But in either case, I stayed at my desk all day, eating my lunch on a tray which was brought to me there. In the evening, I tumbled into bed, telling myself that I simply could not go on like this, that I would have to give up the struggle. But the next day I was back at my desk. There was no other way to meet my obligations.

My birthday occurs in midsummer and for a great many years, whenever I have been at home, I have celebrated it with the same circle of old friends. We had planned an especially festive celebration for that year to mark a significant decade. But when my birthday came, I was thousands of miles from my old friends and the date meant nothing to my new ones. I spent the day alone, and though I wrote, I did so lying on the sofa, because by that time I was too ill to sit at a desk. I was inexpressibly lonely, and when darkness finally fell, my yearning for my own hearthstone and my own people became so acute that the pain of it was almost unbearable. It is one thing, when you are thirty, to forego the associations which mean most to you; there will always be time to renew them later on. It is quite another thing when you are sixty; you know that the sands of time are running low, that precious ties are bound to be broken before long and that no new ones will ever take their place.

Of course my depression was not based on disappointment over missing a festive gathering, but on the realization of what that gathering represented. However, a very real disappointment awaited me: one of my sons, a lieutenant in the Navy, had written me of his happy engagement to a lieutenant in the Army Medical Corps. At that time he was doing port duty in England and she was attached to a hospital in France. They had agreed to be married as soon as either one had leave; if hers came first, she would go to England; if his came first, he would go to

France. Because it was important for me to keep in touch with my foreign publishers and because my next creative writing would logically be done abroad, I had been able to secure a passport and the requisite visas, and I had arranged to attend the wedding ceremony in whichever country it took place. It was celebrated, with all the pomp and circumstance with which the combined services could surround it, at St. James's Church, in Spanish Place, in London. I was still at The Cottage, going from my bed to my sofa and back to bed again and working twelve hours a day on *The River Road*.

The novel was finally finished in September of '45. I did not attempt to pack anything except my clothes. Leaving all the possessions with which I had furnished and equipped The Cottage where they were—which also meant that I had to continue paying rent there—I took a train for New York, intent on sailing for Europe the following week. I had missed my son's wedding, but I was still determined to find out what had happened to my friends in devastated France and I was still bent on writing a book with its scene there. However, for the first time in my career as a writer, the ship on which I had taken passage sailed without me; after I was released from the long-continued strain of working when I was wholly unfit to do so, I collapsed completely. Three weeks went by before

I recovered sufficiently to continue my journey and go home. Most of the autumn was spent in bed and it was not until after the New Year that I could sit at a desk again. I did not get to France until "Spring came around again."

In the meanwhile *The River Road* came out and almost immediately leapt up close to the top of the best seller list. I studied the chart, but it had lost its one-time magic; I told my publisher then that even if the new novel sold a million copies, it would have cost me more than it was worth—in cash and in kind. He laughed and said I would feel differently when it *had* sold a million copies. But I did not. I finally convinced him that I never should.

IV

By the following spring I was well enough to undertake my long-postponed trip to France and, in May, accompanied by Kitty McKiever, a fellow writer and good companion who has shared many of my wanderings, I set sail on a small French freighter named the *Indochinois*.

Transatlantic travel was still prohibited—and rightly so —to all persons who did not have some definite and cogent reason for going abroad. Very few ships were back in service and these few could offer only limited facilities for passengers; accommodations on the Continent were equally scarce and food was considerably scarcer. It was no time to encourage tourist trade, not only for these very sound reasons, but also because visitors, unfamiliar with normal conditions, would inevitably have derived false and unfavorable impressions of the countries and the people they saw. Fortunately for us, Kitty and I did not come into this category; we both had many friends in France whom we were eager to help, a lifelong acquaintance with the country and a thorough knowledge of the language; we both had a definite piece of work to do. We knew that we had been given a great opportunity and we tried to be worthy of it. We did not mind the crowded quarters aboard ship and we were able to accept philosophically the far greater discomforts that awaited us on shore. But those who visualize all foreign travel as a glamorous adventure would certainly have received a series of severe shocks if they had been with us.

We did not go hungry in rural Normandy, though the cities, even in that rich region, were short of food because of transportation difficulties. But we were perpetually cold.

The summer was gray and cheerless and we wore woolen dresses and winter coats all the time. In September the chill of an unseasonably early autumn set in. I had a mild attack of bronchitis, got up too soon and suffered a relapse; after I had repeated this process several times, I became critically ill.

By this time Kitty had gone home and I had been joined by a stoical young secretary, Deanie Bullock. I appreciated her uncomplaining acceptance of the situation, as winter had now begun in dead earnest. For the first time in years, the thermometer in France went down to zero—zero Fahrenheit—and stayed there. In an effort to conserve the wholly inadequate supply of fuel, the government decreed that heat and light should be turned off at seven in the morning and not turned on again until seven at night two days each week. I had been able to secure a room with a fireplace, for which wood, in limited quantities, was available most of the time; and this meant that, even in zero weather, we were better off than most people. But the hours of real daylight, in that latitude, during midwinter, are very short at best—frequently only from ten till three. For at least six hours on such days, the only illumination we had came from our flashlights—until the batteries of these gave out—no new batteries were obtainable—and from the occasional candles which we were able to buy on the black market—none was legally sold at this time. Finally, through the kindness of friends, we secured one antiquated lamp and enough kerosene to keep it lighted through the worst of the darkness. It smoked terribly, it smelled to high heaven and, every time it was used, the room was covered with a black smudge from its fumes. But it sufficed. I had found it very hard to write with only a flashlight or a solitary candle at my disposal; with this smoky kerosene lamp I managed very well.

By January, I was able to sit up a little while each day and, clad in a fur coat and wrapped in blankets, I sat at my desk and went on with my novel, stopping, when my fingers were so numb I could not hold a pencil, to warm them by our little open fire. Even on the days when it was coldest and darkest and I had been sickest, I had not been weighed down with the terrible sense of discouragement and futility that overwhelmed me while I was writing *The River Road*. Somehow I never doubted, this time, that I should be able to finish the work I had undertaken or that it was worth while. The gallant attitude of my secretary and the confidence of my French friends did wonders in the way of keeping up my morale. But though I worked steadily, it was impossible to work fast, and I was beginning to worry about money again.

I had reckoned, when I started abroad, that it would

take me between four and five months to gather my source material and draft my novel; I had now been in France nearly double that time and the end was not yet in sight. I had also reckoned on staying, for the most part, as the paying guest of my friends the Benedictine nuns, at the Monteillerie, near Lisieux, where the cost of living was reasonable. Illness had overtaken me in Paris and even if it had not, the inaccessibility of the Monteillerie in wintertime would have rendered it impractical from the point of view of my work, for conferences with various authorities were increasingly indicated. And the cost of living in Paris was anything but reasonable. Deanie and I had three small rooms facing a courtyard, at a daily basic rate of twenty-seven dollars, which a fifteen per cent service charge and a so-called "luxury tax" brought up to thirty-five. The charge for my breakfast, in American money, was a dollar and a quarter and the contribution of the hotel to my tray consisted of hot water and two pieces of ersatz bread—I supplied Nescafe myself and used saccharine for sweetening; of course there was no milk, but my Norman friends usually managed to send me a little butter; when they could not I went without. Deanie took nothing but tea, which she supplied herself, so, in her case, hot water was the only contribution and this came to a dollar per breakfast tray. Our other meals were correspondingly frugal—

33

and correspondingly expensive; the weekly bills became more and more formidable and more and more disturbing.

My American publisher, according to his habit, had been extremely liberal in the matter of an expense account, calculated to cover a five months' stay abroad; I did not want to ask him for any more money, especially as I realized that, for the second time, I would fail to meet my deadline, and that publication would have to go over from spring until fall. But finally, putting my pride in my pocket, I wrote to my British publisher. He could probably visualize what I was up against, I said frankly. Did he feel that the book on which I was working had enough promise to justify a further advance? His response was immediate and understanding; because of his co-operative attitude, I was able to remain in France until all indicated source material had been gathered and the major part of the drafting done. Late in February I went back to the United States and continued to work intensively on the novel all through the spring. I finished it in June, during the course of a voyage to South America, which unexpectedly turned out to be the next item on my agenda.

V

On my return from France, various questions were put to me about my experiences there and one lady seemed to be especially concerned about the scarcity of food, as it had affected me. Being very wealthy, she did not quite understand why I had been troubled about the high cost of living, and having lived in the Deep South all her life, "zero weather without heat" was simply an expression to her; but she was both puzzled and sympathetic when it came to the subject of table delicacies. "If you did not have any milk," she asked solicitously, "how did you manage about cream?"

I felt and still feel that this question belongs in the same category as the one attributed to Marie Antoinette on the subject of bread and cake. But though it certainly is in a class by itself, as far as those put to me are concerned, there are numerous others which I have found almost equally inane and almost equally irritating. Recently at an (otherwise) delightful dinner, one of my fellow guests, having first informed herself as to the length of my habitual working hours, persistently inquired, "But if you spend so much time at your desk, how do you get in your daily walks?" . . . "I don't take daily walks," I answered. "But you can't be healthy if you don't," the lady went on. I told her I was brought up to believe this, too, and that, as a matter of fact, I was not always conspicuously healthy, though personally I considered lack of exercise a contributing rather than a primary cause of this condition. Undeterred, she labored the subject for some minutes and then went on to another question. "What's more," she said, "I don't see when you take your nap."

Questions of this caliber appear increasingly senseless and become increasingly exasperating because they are asked so often. The average person seems to grasp, without difficulty, the fact that a lawyer, or a doctor, or almost any other professional worker requires years of preparation before he achieves success; also the further fact that it is natural, and, indeed, necessary, for a lawyer to make a habit of trying cases and for a doctor to go on treating patients. But this understanding does not extend to the writing profession; the viewpoint that authors work only when they are "inspired" to do so and that inspiration comes as suddenly and as easily as manna from heaven is so general as to be almost universal. On an average of once a day, unless I lock myself resolutely away from the company of my fellow creatures, I am called upon to explain that books by any established author are written under contract, and that a failure to live up to such a contract not only involves both an author and his publisher in a serious financial loss, as I have said before, but indicates a lack of responsibility and basic good faith. "Then what do you do when you don't feel like writing?" is the question which generally follows the one about inspiration, that has been variously phrased. ("How often do you have an inspiration?" . . . "Did you go to France—or Venezuela—or Japan looking for inspiration?" . . . "Do you just sit around and wait for an inspiration? Etcetera, etcetera.") And when I answer brutally or wearily—depending on how many hours have elapsed since I answered this same question before—that I go on writing anyway, that, as a matter of fact, I seldom feel like doing it, but that, on the other hand, I do like to eat good food and live in a comfortable house and wear nice clothes, my tormentor looks at me incredulously.

"Why, I always supposed that writing was one of your little *diversions!*" a lady recently told me, almost reproachfully, after she had followed up her first question with that other stock query, "Are you planning another book *now?*" and I had answered that I was not only planning one, but writing one, that if I were not, I would be a good deal concerned about the state of my bank account. "You don't mean to say you depend on your writing for money!" she added. And the lady to whom I refer is the wife of a man holding high public office, and is herself well educated, widely acquainted and widely traveled.

"How did you happen to become a writer?" runs another stock question; and when I hesitate, because the reasons for my choice of a career are too complicated for swift and easy explanation, I am urgently admonished to "tell in just a few words." Then there is still another: "Do you have regular hours for writing?" The curt answer, "No, very irregular," is quite apt to give offense; yet, as like as not, the interlocutor has met me on a steamship, or on a railroad train, or in some city far removed from my natural habitat, where my very presence indicates my failure to adhere to a regular routine. At other times I am asked this question by a harassed housewife, who has just finished telling me about her servant troubles, or the vagaries of the carpenter she seeks to employ, or the burden of unexpected company; and when I murmur something about keeping house myself, simultaneously, in several different localities, feeling she will grasp, *ipso facto*, that she and I have the same problems and that she will therefore understand why you find it hard to adhere to an inflexible schedule, she shakes her head unbelievingly. "Well, of course, someone else handles all the troublesome details for *you*," she announces conclusively. And I feel I would rather die than attempt to dispute with her.

But after all, the questions that are asked a writer in person form only a small percentage of the total number he is called upon to answer. Every mail brings in a flood of them; and though their scope reveals a touching confidence in the variety of information at his command, the task of living up to these expectations is a stupendous one. For instance, I find that one correspondent is consulting me on a matter of etiquette; should she write a thank-you note for a shower gift? Though I do not claim to be a second Emily Post, it seems obvious to me that she should, so I answer to that effect. Another correspondent, himself a botanical expert, demands an explanation of a phenomenal fruit tree which adorns the grounds of The Cottage. I am, unfortunately, not a botanical expert myself, so I can only tell him that the tree is where and as I have described it, that I have seen it putting forth both white and crimson flowers, year after year. He is not satisfied with this statement and again demands an explanation. I realize that I must consult authorities at the University of Louisiana and the second letter is temporarily laid aside. Still another correspondent would like to have a temporary home with a "genteel family" in New Orleans, where the total charges for both room and board would not come to more than eight dollars a week. This one is referred, in desperation, to the Chamber of Commerce. The prize problem, as far as expenses were concerned, was presented to me by a correspondent who had five hundred dollars and a six weeks' vacation coming to her and who wanted to visit seven European countries. Would I please supply the itinerary. I am happy to say that, in this instance, I was able to give satisfaction!

In addition to these variegated questions, there are the recurrent ones which must be answered every day as a matter of course. A great many of these are about food. "Will you please send me your favorite recipe for soup—salad—cake—candy?" . . . "Will you please let me know what you are in the habit of eating when you are alone? Also, what you serve when you have company for breakfast—luncheon—afternoon tea—cocktails—dinner—midnight supper?" . . . "What do you consider your most successful menu?" . . . "Do you prefer New England cookery to Southern cookery, or vice versa? Why?" These questions do not present as many difficulties as some of the other kinds, but eventually the process of thinking up another "favorite" becomes a problem, because the term necessarily implies something unique. Moreover, it seems like evading the issue to say that you have no set rule about feeding either yourself or your guests, and that the food of any region can compare favorably with that of any other if it is properly prepared and served.

I can think of only one recent request for a recipe with which it has given me real pleasure to comply and that came from Uganda, East Africa. "We have been reading about mint juleps in *Honor Bright* and *Also the Hills*," wrote my correspondent, "and we think they would taste very good in this climate. Would you be willing to tell us how they are made?" I sent her careful instructions and, in due course, received a grateful acknowledgment; the mint juleps made in Uganda by my recipe had more than come up to expectations. Shortly thereafter I received a similar request from the Transvaal: "We have heard that you have told some of your readers in Uganda how you make mint juleps and we would like to know too." Again I wrote out careful instructions and again I received a grateful acknowledgment. I am deeply gratified to know that, whatever the shortcomings of my novels, they have helped to slake thirst on the Dark Continent!

Requests for biographical material are usually even more urgent than those for recipes. "Our Literary Society is having its regular monthly meeting next Wednesday and YOU are my subject," writes a trustful clubwoman. "I have not had much experience in preparing papers and time is now very short. [It is, indeed!] So by return mail, will you please tell me all about yourself in a way that I can read aloud? Our members will be *simply thrilled* because

41

we are sure you must have had a very *exciting life!!!*" . . .
"Our English Class is taking up the subject of living
authors and I have been given your name," writes a be-
wildered high school student. "But I do not know anything about you. Will you please tell me what books you
have written and why and which ones you consider your
best? I need to know all this right away."

Philip Wylie, in an article entitled "How to Admire
Writers," which appeared in the *Atlantic Monthly,* makes
a comment on the latter type of letter which is the most
apt I have ever seen: "I submit that a man who is concerned with the integrity of his work—who is often driven
by his efforts near to the edge of distraction—and who is
liable to be involved in day-and-night sessions at his desk—
has the right to be somewhat vexed when children are
encouraged thus to invade his privacy. *Teachers do not
urge their pupils to request engineers to stop the locomo-
tives of express trains and tell them all about machinery!* *
Yet the very fact that the request comes from a youngster
gives it special force. Nobody likes to make a kid think
he's been slighted. Because of that, hundreds of American
authors have halted the course of creative activity, some
of them hundreds of times, to help school children with
their lessons."

* The italics are mine.

I wish the simile about the locomotive had occurred to me, for it is the most telling I have ever read and I feel that Mr. Wylie deserves a vote of thanks from all the "distracted authors" who are trying to cope with this type of request; I also think that it would be a wonderful idea to distribute reprints of his whole article, in pamphlet form, by way of answer to such letters. (I have sometimes asked housewives, who insisted on coming to see me when I was in the throes of composition, and who told me they wanted to take up "just fifteen minutes of my valuable time," what would happen to an angel cake if they removed it from the oven for fifteen minutes when it was half-done and then put it back again. But I have never been rewarded by anything but a blank stare in answer to this question; the housewives could not see the connection between an interrupted angel cake and an interrupted story.)

Mr. Wylie also points out that, apparently, the high school children—and may I add, the club women!—never consult *Who's Who* or any other standard work of reference; apparently, they never visualize an author's working schedule as being so crowded that it provides very little leeway to cope with such requests; and, apparently, they never take into consideration either the possible necessity of forwarding mail and the amount of time inevitably consumed in getting their letters into an errant author's hands! With all the good will in the world, it is impossible to give such communications the immediate and detailed attention expected; and they are supplemented by others of still a different ilk, which are even harder to answer. These come from would-be or embryonic authors, who ask for help and advice and often enclose scripts which they would like to have read, edited and submitted to a publisher. Many of them suggest collaboration on terms which recall President Coolidge's recipe for a horse and rabbit pie. ("One horse to one rabbit.") They know a wonderful story, based on real life, but they do not know how to write it. If I would undertake this trifling task, they would be glad to share the proceeds with me, on a fifty-fifty basis. Many others feel that there is some kind of a magic formula for becoming a successful author, and still others that it is all a matter of "pull," that, if you know the "right people," you can get anything published. I take special pains to answer all these letters, because I have not forgotten that, when I was a beginner myself, there was no one to whom I could appeal; I vowed at the time that if I were ever in a position to help another novice who was in the same state of bewilderment and discouragement, I would not turn a deaf ear. But most of the would-be authors who appeal to me are hard to help.

Either they have not that little God-given spark we call talent, without which no amount of work will do any good; or else they have it and are not willing to work, and without work, the talent is no use either; it might just as well be folded away in a napkin, like the one we read about in the Bible.

Necessarily, I am less responsive to requests—or demands—for money than I am to appeals for help with manuscripts; if I were not, I would soon be completely bankrupt. They come from all over the world, and they range all the way from petitions by Indian fanatics to pleas for support while exploring the realms of the more obscure arts. One man wrote that he had caused a large picture to be painted as the result of a vision and needed six thousand dollars to further the cult of this painting; another, that he had not visited Louisiana in twenty years and felt the time was ripe to do so again, but that, unfortunately, funds—which he was sure I would be glad to supply— were lacking. Needless to say, demands of this sort are automatically refused—as are all requests for photographs. (A separate fund, completely out of proportion to my budget, would have to be created to pay for the latter by the gross.) But cases of real need do receive consideration and, to the limits of my resources, some kind of a modest response.

Of course all letters do not contain questions and petitions; some merely contain comments; and though the great majority of these comments are pleasant, others are extremely disagreeable. It is easy enough to say that you should not permit yourself to be cast down by such remarks, that they probably come from cranks and bigots; but it is sometimes hard to follow this sound advice. An unjustly critical or abusive letter, received when its recipient is exhausted, discouraged or battling against illness and trouble, can do a great deal of real harm by increasing a writer's depression and robbing him of his self-confidence. For instance, whenever I receive a letter taking issue with me as a Catholic, I wonder why I have failed in my sincere endeavors to live up to my religion and worry because I am not more of a credit to my chosen church. Most other kinds I can dismiss more lightly. It does not trouble me very much when I am accused of being subsidized by the liquor interests, because of my references to those mint juleps which have given so much pleasure in Uganda; the charge is too ridiculous on the face of it. I have also ceased to take very much to heart the suggestions that I should have used a semicolon instead of a comma or vice versa and the sharp rebukes for certain similes. (One correspondent reproved me for causing a character to remark, jokingly, that his hungry companion was acting "like a starving Armenian"—on the ground that it showed racial prejudice!) I do not worry too much, either, when I am told that a reader has burnt a book because of "improper love scenes," though once or twice I have written back to inquire which scenes these were, only to receive very vague replies. One letter that I actually cherish found fault with both the drinking habits and the amorous inclinations of my characters. "You should write a book that has nothing about either drinking or sex in it," the writer admonished me. "Neither would ever be missed in real life." I am still wondering whether this correspondent, who was evidently a mature woman—indeed, the word Mrs. appeared before her name in parentheses—has an unshakable belief in storks.

Though the daily mail always presents a problem, this problem becomes doubly acute when it involves books instead of letters. Long ago, I saw the wisdom of investing in autograph slips, already prepared for pasting, adorned with my initials and bearing the inscription, "With Best Wishes from the Author." It takes only a couple of minutes to add a signature and send such a slip on its way and the recipient of this trifling attention is, apparently, always pleased with it. But alas! many correspondents, instead of first asking for autographs and then awaiting results, trustfully send out their books. Books do not come in the category of first-class mail and, consequently, are not automatically forwarded; but almost as if with malice and forethought, they are addressed to me in New Hampshire when I am in New Orleans, and vice versa, and practically anywhere in the United States when I am in Europe or South America. Eventually, irate letters concerning these books catch up with me. What have I done with the precious volume that was sent me two months earlier? Return postage was enclosed. [This, as a matter of fact, is rare.] Am I using the stamps, besides keeping the novel? Deanie and I make valiant efforts to track down the missing volume, appealing to an unresponsive post office and searching a long-unoccupied house; if our efforts prove futile, we replace the book. But we do not seem to make friends that way and we certainly do not make money.

The craze for autographs has reached such proportions that an author may well be pardoned for deciding that the only escape from collectors of these is in the grave. The last time I went to France, I had hardly reached my room in the small hotel at Cherbourg where I spent my first night ashore, before a bevy of school children appeared with grimy slips of paper in their hands and expectant expressions on their smiling faces. Of course I could not send them disappointed away. On a still more recent trip to Venezuela, it seemed as if I could never stop at the desk

of my hotel to get my mail, or sit down in the lounge for a quiet chat with friends, that some total stranger did not come sidling up to me. On shipboard, it was even worse; I kept as much as possible to my stateroom, but when I emerged for a refreshing drink before dinner, someone was lying in wait for me at the bar. The climax came very late one night, when I was roused from my first sound sleep by a terrific pounding on the door. I threw on a dressing gown and hastened to answer, sure that some frightful emergency must have arisen. Before me stood an apologetic steward with an autograph book in his hand.

"I am afraid it is a little on the late side," he said, "but I was told you wouldn't mind signing this. The lady it belongs to has heard that sometimes you write cute little verses too. She thought if I left this with you till morning, maybe you'd favor her with some.'

VI

Reviewers, no less than correspondents and autograph hunters, can have an extremely depressing effect on a conscientious author. I have long since accepted the fact that I shall never win critical acclaim and, though of course I should have liked to be worthy of it, especially since it was originally my hope to be regarded as a woman of letters rather than as a best-selling author, I have resigned myself, more or less philosophically, to the latter role. Adverse reviews, however disappointing and damaging to one's pride, can also be philosophically accepted if and when they are, in some measure, fair and, to some degree, based on fact; it is when they are unjust and inaccurate that they hurt. "Her character [that of the heroine] emerges smoothly from Mrs. Keyes's fast moving typewriter," says a Richmond reviewer, calmly taking it for granted that I write in a rapid, effortless fashion and that I use a typewriter. Alas! I have never done and never shall do the former. (The passages in question were drafted and redrafted at least twenty times.) And it is twenty-five years now since physical disabilities first prevented me from doing the latter. "The complete disregard for good literary form in this book is lamentable," writes a Nashville reviewer. "But then Mrs. Keyes has never cared whether she wrote good English." Never *cared!* There has been nothing about which I cared more, nothing I have tried harder to do. Apparently, I have failed, even though some of my books are now required reading at certain colleges. I must

try harder, I will, indeed. But to say I do not *care*! . . .
"The fine old restaurant will doubtless survive the insult
offered it," scathingly writes a New Orleans reviewer. The
insult? I thought I was paying it a compliment when I used
its name. The proprietor thought so too, or at least he assured me he did, not once but many times; otherwise of
course I would not have done it. But another Orleanian,
who ought to be in a position to know, pronounces my
title an insult to an ancient and honorable institution. . . .
"Mrs. Keyes who comes from Crowley, is naturally so
dazzled by the bright lights of New Orleans that she cannot see the city as it really is," opines a small-town Texas
critic. Perhaps I do not see the city as it really is, but this
cannot be because I come from Crowley. Though I am
very fond of that pleasant place, I never saw it until four
years ago, and that was after more than thirty years' residence in world capitals. It is a long, long time since I have
been dazzled by bright lights—in fact, I have grown very
weary of them. Another reviewer—a Carolinian this time
—does not credit me with coming from Louisiana, but
states that I have spent most of my time there "since
1912." This was a source of surprise to everyone who
knows me, but especially to my youngest son, who claims
he has always been given to believe, on reliable authority,
that he was born in Boston that year and that his mother

was present on this occasion. He further states that his earliest memories seem to center around Pine Grove Farm and Concord in New Hampshire, his slightly later ones around Washington, D. C., and that his mother is very much a part of these also. Even after he went away to school and college and became a teacher and himself the head of a family he continued to visit her in Alexandria, Virginia, at Pine Grove Farm and in Newbury, Vermont; but he has never been to Louisiana. In other words, the reviewer's date is something more than thirty years out of the way. But I suppose we should not be too captious about minor inaccuracies. . . . "Mrs. Keyes has forsaken her usual field of historical fiction, which is rather a pity; she does better with her costume novels." This comment, which comes both from my native state of Virginia and my favorite New York paper, seems, in a way, the unkindest cut of all, for I have never written a costume novel! It is all too evident that the reviewer has been misled by the title, *Came a Cavalier,* and that he has not looked inside the covers of that or any other book of mine. If I am fated to be condemned by an authority who will not even take the trouble to see whether I deserve his low opinion, then this is an aspect of authorship which I find it hard to accept with good grace.

VII

Another aspect of authorship which I find extremely trying is based on the fact that so many persons are convinced that certain characters in my novels are drawn from real life. Apparently, nothing can shake this conviction. Over and over again, I have tried to explain that, since certain emotions and experiences are part of the human lot, those which I ascribe to imaginary characters may very well be the same that Susan Smith and John Jones have had; and, since I am trying to make my characters as lifelike as possible, their reactions to these experiences and emotions will—I hope—be presented as similar to Miss Smith's and Mr. Jones's. Moreover—as I also patiently reiterate—there are only a certain number of possible physical characteristics and the different combinations of circumstances which can be effected are also necessarily limited; it would be strange if, sooner or later, a novelist did not happen to hit on one or the other which came within the realm of the reader's observation or acquaintance. Even the names which a novelist plucks from the air, as being suited, for one reason or another, to his characters, must necessarily approximate or even duplicate the names of real persons, since these are also limited.

I shall never forget the terrible sensation that overcame me the day after the publication of my second novel, entitled *The Career of David Noble,* when I beheld, lying on top of my morning mail, a communication with the imposing letterhead, "David Noble and Sons, Attorneys at Law"! I was sure that I must have unwittingly given offense and that I was confronted with the charge of libel! As it turned out, my fears were entirely groundless. The writer had seen the announcement of my book, had bought it, read it and enjoyed it; but his curiosity was aroused: how had I happened to name my hero David Noble? The reason he asked was because he himself was the sixth David Noble in a direct line.

Fortunately, this gentleman believed me when I told him that my choice of a name had been wholly accidental; and, in two other cases, where I had hit on the names of real persons, they have been equally pleasant about it and equally ready to believe that I was telling the truth. (Once, when a book had already advanced as far as page proof, *six* names were changed in it because I discovered, in the nick of time, that I had used real ones and these persons could not possibly have been pleased, because my characters, in this instance, were the villains of the piece!) But sometimes people continue to shake their heads and smile incredulously when I assure them that I have never consciously put a living person in a story without his knowledge, consent and approval.

Not long ago, I went out to supper with some friends who felt sure I would enjoy the small restaurant where they had discovered an especially fine form of crayfish bisque. We were hardly seated when an occupant of an adjacent table joined us and asked for five autographs; she repeated her visit three times and each time lingered longer than she had the time before; our original plan for a quietly congenial meal was completely disrupted, but that, as I have already said, is a more or less common occurrence. Somewhat discouraged, however, we prepared to leave the restaurant as soon as we had finished our crayfish, to continue our visit at home; but my progress was blocked by a diner from still another table.

"I have been wanting to tell you for some time," he informed me, "that I know who you had in mind when you created the character of Raoul Bienvenu in *Crescent Carnival*."

Genuinely startled, I replied that the formation of the "Bayou Battalion," attributed in this novel to Raoul Bienvenu was—as nearly everyone in Louisiana is well aware —really the accomplishment of my friend, Captain Robert Mouton. He himself had given me permission to fictionize this dramatic exploit and it was so stated in the Foreword.

Otherwise, *as far as I knew,* nothing about Raoul Bien-venu's career bore any resemblance to that of an actual Marine officer; certainly it bore no resemblance to Bob's. The gentleman who had stopped me continued to smile, to shake his head and to reiterate that, of course, I would have to say this, but he knew. . . . I was finally rescued by Deanie who, with her usual resourcefulness, came to say that our car was blocking traffic. But my feeling of helplessness, tinged with distress, persisted all that night. Personally, I have less use for a liar than for almost any other kind of contemptible creature. Why should I be condemned to be bracketed in a class which I myself so thoroughly despise? As a matter of fact, I do not think my word would be questioned if, for instance, I made a positive statement about my financial standing or my religious faith. Why then, should it be questioned in regard to my writing? This, as I have said before, is a trust as well as a trade, which I would no more dream of misrepresenting than I would think of saying I had a thousand dollars in the bank if I were actually overdrawn, or of denying the divinity of Our Lord, while approaching the Communion rail.

Sometimes this mistaken conviction that I have portrayed real characters has very far-reaching consequences. In one of my books, I presented, as a minor character, a conscientious and industrious, but rather tactless and aggressive, clubwoman; it is a type that is found everywhere in the United States. My honest answer, if I were asked who had suggested this character to me, would be that I did not know, because I had met such women all the way from Maine to California. I assume that Helen Hokinson must have done so too, or we never would have had the series of remarkable drawings, which have been so deservedly popular and in which she so excelled and which, as far as I know, have never given offense to anyone. But a certain prominent woman decided that I was holding her up to ridicule and neither she nor her family has ever forgiven me for the imagined aspersions cast upon her. More than one extremely unpleasant episode has resulted from this baseless ill will.

In another instance, I described a certain man as having "grizzled" hair, and, in this case, a real name was used, for the man, long since dead, played a prominent role in the bygone era I was describing. Since then, I have read a description of the great Italian tenor, Ezio Pinza, by Robert Ruark, in which he says, "As Emil de Becque, the tropic isle planter [in *South Pacific*], Mr. Pinza has stirred forgotten emotions among the matrons and has dignified grizzled hair to the acute embarrassment of forty-year-old juveniles." I have also noticed several references to highly respected Irish-Americans of advancing years as "grizzled" in Henry Morton Robinson's *Cardinal*. As far as I know, neither Mr. Ruark nor Mr. Robinson has been reproached or misunderstood on this score; and no dictionary which I have ever consulted and no colloquialism with which I was hitherto familiar give more than one meaning to this adjective: "Somewhat gray; grayish." I did, and do, readily say that my own hair is grizzled and that of most of my contemporary friends; we have reached the age when it "belongs to be"—to borrow a phrase of the Deep South. But, evidently, some persons in the Deep South are not willing to abide by dictionary definitions, or else they use colloquialisms which exist nowhere else; at all events, a hue and cry went up: in describing his hair as grizzled, I had intimated that this prominent personage had colored blood! Aghast at the turn things had taken, I disclaimed all intention of having made a charge which—as common sense alone would be sufficient to tell me—would demonstrate a lack of tact that would hurt me far more than it could possibly hurt anyone else in this region. But I might have sworn this on a stack of Bibles, as well as a stack of dictionaries. It would have made no difference.

Even inanimate objects are not safe from the obsession that their fictional use has an association with real persons of whom the author has probably never even heard. The most striking example of this which has made trouble for me is in connection with a hand mirror of my mother's, which I admired from childhood and which I long felt should find a fictional place in a novel. My mother, the only daughter of an only daughter of an only daughter—as I was myself—inherited a great many beautiful things, partly because there was no one with whom to divide these legacies, and partly because her mother, her grandmother and her great-grandmother were all luxury-loving New Yorkers, possessed of the wherewithal to indulge their taste for silverware, jewelry, paintings, *objets d'art,* rare furs and fine laces. The men in their lives vied with each other in adding to their stock of personal adornments and household equipment, and apparently they had generous suitors, adoring husbands—two or more if they were widowed early—and devoted sons. By the time I came along, my mother was in a position to offer me the exciting privilege of "choosing" from several well-stocked jewel boxes which ornament would best suit the new Paris dress into which she was being hooked while preparing for a party; and, after her hairdresser and her maid had completed their ministrations and stood back to survey the work of their hands with admiration, she invariably picked up her silver hand mirror, which was studded with rose diamonds, and surveyed herself with pardonable satisfaction.

As I look back, I wonder why it never occurred to me to write a story set in that sumptuous bedroom of a huge house on Beacon Street. The scene would have contained massive mahogany furniture, upholstery of rose-colored brocade and drawn draperies of Brussels lace. It would have been peopled with Miss Neal, the meek, shabby little hairdresser, who scurried from the service of one fashionable lady to that of another and whose only pride lay in the elaborate structures of braids and ringlets which she created and crowned with velvet bows, satin roses, nodding plumes and jeweled circlets; with Ella, the comely maid, her fluted cap and full apron both stiff with starch; with the excited little girl bounding up and down in the middle of a big bed and surrounded by open jewel boxes whose contents were strewn over the Marseilles spread; and with the vain, charming woman, seated before her dressing table, holding her diamond-studded mirror in one white hand, while with the other she gave the final touch to the laces on her breast or straightened the chain of the necklace at her throat.

I can still feel the firelight which gave a touch of warmth and coziness to the formal elegance of that room; I can still hear Miss Neal and Ella murmuring admiration; I can still smell the heliotrope perfume which my mother dabbled lightly behind her ears; and I can still see her, laying down the mirror, picking up her long white gloves and her bunch of violets and then, after kissing me good night, sweeping off to meet my stepfather, who would be waiting for her downstairs, immaculate in evening dress, his opera cape thrown back from his shoulders, his tall silk hat deferentially held in his hand. When she had gone, the room which she had left in a state of lavish disorder would be put to rights, the garments she had discarded consigned to the laundry basket or hung carefully in the closet; the jewelry replaced in the velvet trays of the jewel boxes; the Marseilles spread removed and folded, the sheets turned down in neat triangles over the blankets; the long-sleeved cambric nightgown, adorned with tucks and featherstitching, the pink cashmere wrapper, likewise tucked and featherstitched, laid on top of them. And while Ella attended to all of this—Miss Neal having already scurried away to her next patroness—the little girl continued to finger her mother's mirror until her governess—a prim spinster named Miss Charlotte Jones, whose high, boned collars were always fastened with a pansy pin—came in to say reproachfully, "Why, Frances, you know you were supposed to come straight back to the nursery as soon as your dear mamma and your dear papa had gone out to dinner. . . ."

Well, the fact remains that I never did write about all

this before. But, after a long mental search for just the right place to put it, I saw that mirror as a very logical Carnival favor. So, in imagination, I transferred it from my own dressing table, which it now adorns, to the Ball of the Twelfth Night Revelers, where a wholly imaginary hero presented it, somewhat surreptitiously, to a wholly imaginary heroine—it being rather too valuable to give openly. After that, it played quite a prominent part in the story of my chief characters and that of their descendants and, because of this and also because it is essentially photogenic, it was reproduced on the jacket of the book. Several years later, to my great amazement, a visitor at my house picked it up, gazed at it sorrowfully and went through the motions of wiping away a tear.

"No doubt you enjoy using this mirror," she said with a deep sigh. "But I cannot help feeling sorry for the poor people who lost it."

"Nobody ever lost it," I said, still grappling with my astonishment. "My mother used it constantly—it was given her when I was about four years old. When she died, it was put away in a safe-deposit vault and kept there until the estate was settled. But there was never any question that she had left it to me and I have used it ever since—except when I am traveling, of course. Then I put it in my own safe-deposit box."

My visitor shook her head. "Naturally you would have to say that," she remarked sadly. (The observation was exactly the same, you see, as the one made by the gentleman who told me he knew whom I had in mind when I created Raoul Bienvenu.) "But I happen to know the poor Creole lady from whom you bought it—for a fraction of what it was worth. I even know the jeweler who designed it for her. It was one of the few important pieces she had left from the wreckage of her fortune and her most precious treasure. Besides, it had a great sentimental value to her—as you are well aware, since you told the story of that. I suppose a novelist never regards any confidence as sacred; but you might have at least paid my poor friend properly for her mirror."

Such unjust accusations, hurled at an author about the integrity of his work, are as deeply resented—and rightly —as accusations against the integrity of his character, for his work is part of his character, though the average layman does not realize this; and because of such righteous resentment, unjust accusations can really be very dangerous—to the one who makes them. It is no idle saying that the pen is mightier than the sword. Writers have a very powerful weapon of retaliation in their hands and sometimes the temptation to use it proves too powerful to resist. There are several classic examples of this and of the havoc it has wrought. I must confess that I have had to fight this temptation over and over again, myself; so far, I have never succumbed to it. I hope and pray that I never shall.

VIII

In the last analysis, there are no circumstances under which an author is at the public's mercy more completely than when he is autographing books at a store. It is possible to leave a restaurant, or almost any kind of a private party, if a situation becomes unbearable. But once an author has agreed to autograph books, for a certain length of time, and a store has made arrangements for him to do so and published advertisements, saying that he will, nothing short of battle, murder and sudden death can deliver him from his torment. I do not mean to infer, of course, that all such engagements represent endurance tests; sometimes they are very pleasant and very profitable. But the author has got to face the fact that they may not be and he has got to grin and bear it if they are not.

When the director of a bookstore or a book department

has the situation well in hand, he or she will see to it that the author is not badgered or browbeaten; however, cranks are an integral part of any large crowd and so are spongers. Over and over again, a long line of would-be purchasers is held up by some woman—I am sorry to say that it generally is a woman—who has not the slightest intention of buying a book, but who has seized the opportunity of telling the author everything that is wrong with what he has written, or asking him innumerable questions about both his personal and professional life. Very often, the diatribes begin with the statement: "You don't remember me, do you? Why, I met you in 1923 at a reception in Washington!" The poor author, who probably met several hundred other persons at that same reception and who has met many thousands since, tries, conscientiously but vainly, to place his persecutor, who, bridling with hurt pride, goes off at another tangent, much more devastating. Meanwhile, besides the would-be purchasers, two or three critical observers, who have stationed themselves at a near-by vantage point, are making very personal remarks in stage whispers: "Well, I never supposed writers looked like *that*. . . . Do you really believe it's true? I mean—you know. . . ."

Again, would-be purchasers are delayed, not by individuals, but by groups. Sometimes as many as sixty teen-agers, armed with autograph books, but no cash, arrive in a body. The director of the book department cannot bid them begone, because, very probably, their parents buy can openers or shaving cream or some such commodity in another department and their good will is important to the store as a whole. But the youngsters can very effectively block a day's sales and reduce an author to a state of complete exhaustion.

Robert Tallant, whom I know and greatly like, says that when he goes to autograph books in a department store, the first woman who comes up to his little table asks him the way to the corset department and the next one the way to the ladies' room. After that, he sometimes sells a book. I must confess that no man has ever asked me correlative questions. But I have been asked practically everything else, though sometimes I, too, eventually sell a book.

IX

The effort of coping with the purchasing (?) public on such occasions is, as I have tried to indicate, great enough

to constitute a full-time job temporarily, at least from my point of view. But I find that, in addition to autographing books, which has been stipulated and agreed upon beforehand; and answering questions, which, in a certain sense, is all in the day's work, I am also very frequently constrained to pose for photographs, to give interviews, and to make tape recordings, to be used in connection with that pet project of publishers and their collaborators known as PUBLICITY. (Or, if they are trying to be especially tactful and tender with an author, as "promotional activity" or as "a phase of public relations.")

I have never liked to have my picture taken for general use, partly because I was brought up in the belief that no lady ever permitted anyone except her nearest and dearest to possess a likeness of her—a belief closely allied to the one, also traditional in my family, which precluded the appearance of her name in the public prints except on three occasions: her birth, her marriage and her death. When I married a man who figured prominently on the national scene, I was, unavoidably, obliged to depart from the letter of this law; but I never wholly departed from the spirit of it, even when I achieved a career of my own. However, my reluctance at having my photograph appear here, there and everywhere was somewhat mitigated by the fact that, in those days, it was reasonably attractive. Inevitably, as I grew older, it became less so; and the time arrived when, without being unduly vain—or so I hope and believe—I shrank from having the clumsiness which is an integral part of my physical handicap revealed to pitiless public gaze. I have tried, over and over again, to explain this shrinking without making a mountain out of a molehill; so far, I have never once succeeded, even when I have stipulated beforehand that no photographs should be taken in connection with scheduled activities. I do not blame the photographers for this; they must go where they are sent and do what they are told to do; and heaven knows —I do too—that a news photographer, operating by flashlight and compelled to get the product of his camera into the next edition of his paper, cannot turn out the same sort of work as the artist with different equipment and more time at his disposal. Besides, the news photographer is further hampered by the requirement of a stereotyped form of presentation.

"Now, Mrs. Keese, if you will just be looking at this book with the lady on your left! Hold it between you, but don't bend over too far—it hides your face. Don't turn toward the camera either, turn toward each other. And keep saying something, it doesn't matter what. We want to show you as if you were talking about the book. Fine! Hold it!"

72

How many times I have heard that and conscientiously "held it," cringing at every word, because I knew what the results would be—the wholly unnatural position which exaggerates every defect of face and figure, the terrible profiles, the gaping mouths, the silly smiles!

During rationing, when I could not get gasoline enough for my car, some photographs, showing me in a wheel chair, being transferred from train to train, were widely circulated. They were unprepossessing, to say the least; but they did have the merit of authenticity: I really was crippled, I really was trying to carry on my work under a handicap; and though I would have vastly preferred not to have this publicized, I did not mind it half so much as I mind being held up to ridicule under a guise which has no basis in normal action and, therefore, nothing to justify it.

The news photographer seldom arrives alone. Lurking behind him is the reporter, pad and pencil in hand. Again, let me say this is a case where the perpetrator of the deed should not be blamed for what he is doing. He belongs, almost invariably, to the group that has been caught young, treated rough and told nothing. Only a few great cosmopolitan papers pay an author the real tribute of having him interviewed by an expert, under advantageous circumstances, and giving him a chance to correct any inadvertent errors which the interviewer may have committed. Any author would be pleased and proud to be interviewed by Harvey Breit, Fanny Butcher, J. Donald Adams or Alice Dixon Bond, for instance. But such complimentary gestures are, alas! few and far between; and most city editors apparently send out their representatives at such top speed that the poor cubs get no briefing whatsoever on their prospective victims. At a recent private reception, given to celebrate the publication of a new book, the photographers had hardly finished their deadly work when a reporter came up to me with the question, "This is your first book of nonfiction, isn't it?" Not wishing to give the effect of rebuking him, I refrained from saying, "No, it is my tenth," and simply replied, "No"—which, of course, sounded abrupt and unco-operative. "How did you happen to write it?" he next inquired. By this time, a dozen or more guests were waiting to greet me and, without being really discourteous to them, it was impossible for me to withdraw from the receiving line long enough to enter into a dissertation on the side. "Didn't I explain that in the Prologue?" I asked, rather desperately.

"Oh, I haven't seen the *book*," the reporter exclaimed ingenuously, "I just have to see *you*."

My most trying experience of this type occurred in connection with a speech which I had agreed to make at a

74

large university, in the course of the commencement exercises. A few days before it was scheduled to take place, I became violently ill and wired to the Chairman of the Program Committee, asking to be released from the engagement. She replied that it was impossible to find a substitute at such a late date and besought me to make the effort to come. I finally wrung a reluctant consent from my physician, coupled with the condition that I should not be required to give any interviews or engage in any extraneous activities—indeed, that I should go to bed as soon as I arrived at my destination, stay there until it was time to make my speech and then go back to bed until I started for home. These conditions were accepted. But, on my arrival, I was met at the airport not only by my hostess, but by a photographer and two reporters. I had had no lunch; I was tired, empty and in considerable pain; and, as politely as I could, I explained the circumstances, reviewed the conditions under which I had come and asked to be excused. Not a word that I said had the slightest effect; it was soon evident that unless I created a scene in a public place, I could not escape. Slumped down on a hard bench, I was duly photographed; and while airplanes roared overhead, I tried to answer "in just a few words" the questions which have been asked so many hundreds of times already and to which it is literally impossible to reply without

75

quiet, leisure and a composed mind. At last I eluded my persecutors, motored to the beautiful house where I was to stay and reached my own room; but almost immediately my hostess knocked at the door: the representative of a rival paper felt very much injured because she had not been included in the interview, so, if I would not mind too much. . . . I did mind and said so, still trying to do it pleasantly; but the representative of the rival paper was already on her way to the house. She did not leave it until two hours later. I had no supper until after eight and I did not get to bed until after midnight.

It is probably unnecessary to add that the aftermath of this rashly undertaken trip was a very uncomfortable week in bed, where I could not escape from the reproaches heaped upon me by my physician, my secretary and my housekeeper for my folly in having kept the engagement. During the intervals between these reproaches, I "read, marked, learned and inwardly digested" the articles which had appeared as the result of the interviews at the airport. They were extremely caustic in character and, at first, I was inclined to resent them as unjust, for I have never been consciously unfair or discourteous to anyone in my life. Then I realized that they had served a useful purpose: they had proven, beyond the last shadow of a doubt, that I should not make any more speeches.

To be sure, I had come to this conclusion before, only to weaken afterward. One of the occasions when I decided my career as a speaker should end arose when my train deposited me, some distance from the station platform, at 2:00 A.M., in the midst of a raging blizzard. No one had come to meet me and there were no taxis in sight. I dragged my suitcases, one by one, through the snow to the platform, telephoned from a pay station in the waiting room, and eventually secured a cab, which finally took me to a drab and dreary hotel. The bellboy, who carried my bags to a bleak room, looked at me askance when I asked him if he could not get me a hot drink from a near-by drugstore; it appeared that there *were* no near-by drug-stores, and that, even if there had been, none would still be open at such an hour. The linen room in the hotel was closed too, of course, and there was only one blanket on the lumpy bed. I got into it with all my clothes on and shivered through what remained of the night. My teeth were still chattering when I rose to address the complacent club members who had summoned me to Wisconsin in midwinter.

Another occasion arose when, on fifteen minutes' notice, I agreed to take the place of a speaker, who had been prevented by bad weather from flying to Washington in time to address an Authors' Breakfast. This was when *The*

River Road was occupying a gratifying place on the best seller list and I thought that some of the experiences I have just set down about my two years at The Cottage, told in a more or less jesting vein, might amuse the audience. Evidently I was right, as far as the majority of my hearers was concerned, for laughter seemed spontaneous, applause was hearty and I received a large number of fan letters from persons who had listened in on the radio. (The speech was broadcast over a major hookup.) But one of my listeners was angered by what she considered a disparagement of her native state. Instead of voicing enjoyment, like the other persons who approached me after the speech was over, she began by asking me in tones of rage why I did not go back to my native New England and write books insulting that part of the country. I tried to explain that, though I was not a native of New England, I was very fond of it, and had already written numerous books about it which, as far as I had ever heard, no one there considered insulting; also that I had certainly not meant to insult Louisiana either. (It is a curious thing that New England seems to rather enjoy having a little gentle fun poked at it, whereas the Deep South is apt to take umbrage at even an imagined criticism. I have often wondered why this is.) Without giving me a chance to finish, my accuser exclaimed furiously, "Well it certainly is a

good thing for you that we don't shoot skunks down in Louisiana. If we did, you'd have been dead and buried long ago!"

The memory of this attack rankled, I must confess, for some time. It hurt the more, I suppose, because I really thought I had done a good deed in pinch-hitting for an absent author and filling in the serious gap which would have otherwise appeared on the program; and because no one connected with this program stepped forward to defend me. I have since then declined to appear under the same auspices again. But, as I said before, in spite of such experiences, I occasionally permitted myself to be over-persuaded as far as other speeches were concerned—until I had the experience of the correlative obligations at the university commencement. It was those, and nothing to do with the speech—which, indeed, passed off very pleasantly in that instance—or with any other speech, however unpleasant in itself, which finally defeated me. The cost of those correlative obligations—which are also correlatives of writing best sellers, since it is in this connection that a writer is featured on such occasions—is really too high.

X

Among these correlative obligations, the one which constrains an author to accept and extend innumerable invitations to social functions ranks very high also. I have never had any desire to dwell in an ivory tower of isolation. I am a gregarious human being, "given to hospitality" myself and likewise receptive to it. I am fond of being with old friends and happy to make new ones; and I consider that the prevalence of both old friends and new, in many different parts of the globe, has contributed very greatly to my personal pleasure and my professional success. Indeed, I have often found that even the most casual acquaintances, encountered in the course of a trip or at some hospitable home, have proven not only extremely congenial, but extremely enlightening and extremely helpful. However, there are limits to the number of parties which I have the physical strength to attend in any given period, without an aftermath of prostrating fatigue; and still greater limits to the number of persons whom I can enjoy, or to whose enjoyment I feel I can add, at any one time; and it is literally impossible for me to come home and go back to my desk, for long hours of intensive work, after appearing at festive occasions where too much food, too much liquor, too much smoke and too much noise have all entered into the picture. Neither my brain nor my body is equal to such an ordeal.

Even if it were, I should still feel that the most propitious time for good fellowship is almost invariably at the end of a day's work and not before it begins or in the middle of it. I do not think it matters very much whether the occasion provides a cup of tea, a highball, a simple supper or a feast fit for the gods if the more essential elements to make it pleasant are not lacking—in fact, a "dinner of herbs" is still better, to my way of thinking, than a "stalled ox," as it was in Biblical times, if the first is served lovingly and the second has "hatred therewith." But I never can and never could face philosophically the prospect of being dragged out of bed to make merry at an early morning breakfast or sitting through a typical ladies' luncheon in the middle of the day or of screaming myself hoarse at a crowded cocktail party in the afternoon. When I find that I am expected to do all three of these things between sunrise and sunset, my feeling of collapse sets in before I have even started on my rounds, just as surely as my sensation that a dental chair is the least comfortable seat in the world begins as soon as I set foot in the outer office.

I should perhaps confess that I am one of those persons to whom breakfast, even with my nearest and dearest, has no attractions; that the ideal way to begin a day, as far as I am concerned, is to turn over in bed, ring a bell and joyously, though drowsily, await the arrival of very strong, very hot coffee. This perquisite is one of the most precious which advancing years and moderate prosperity have earned for me. As a schoolgirl I rose early and, as a young mother, my working day often began at 4:00 A.M. (It now not infrequently ends at that hour; but, in my opinion, this is much the lesser of two evils.) My mother, a lady of leisurely habits which I failed to fully appreciate in my youth, had early been exposed to Continental customs and believed in breakfasting not only late, but lightly and casually. Though the requirements of an inflexible school schedule obliged me to rise early, she did nothing of the sort herself; nor did she see to it that I was fortified with anything more substantial than rolls and *café au lait*—less and less *lait* and more and more *café* as I mounted higher and higher on the ladder of the teens—with which to face the roster of Saxon kings or to travel vicariously over the parasangs by which the army described by Xenophon advanced.

It was not until after my marriage that I became acquainted with what I believe is generally known as a "typical American breakfast"; and though I do remember that fresh fruit in season, hot cereal with sugar and cream, eggs in various forms, buttered toast, muffins, doughnuts and, very frequently, sausages and griddlecakes were all provided at my mother-in-law's bountiful table, I never appreciated these delicacies at the hour when they were offered, and the ceremony which attended them was overwhelming to me. At seven-thirty in the morning, the assembled family, all fully and rather formally dressed, gathered around a large table, and an immaculate damask cloth, fine English porcelain, and a complete silver service were all taken as a matter of course. So was a rosy-cheeked Swedish maid, dressed in stiffly starched percale, who changed the plates every few minutes as course succeeded course; and every amenity of polite conversation was scrupulously observed, even if this proceeded at a dignified, rather than a lively pace.

Candor compels me to state that I found the effort of trying to live up to these breakfasts very exhausting and that, though this effort was sincere, it was never very successful. Before many years had passed, my husband's family accepted the fact that my reprehensible upbringing did not qualify me for early morning heartiness and that I had no adequate code of etiquette for matutinal behavior. As soon as my youngest child had departed for boarding school, I joyously abandoned all pretense of "getting up in good season." It remained for the reading public and its confederates to accomplish what no one else had ever been able to achieve.

It was, I found, taken for granted that when I visited in strange cities, I would wish to begin my acquaintance with them and their inhabitants early in the day. (Strange *cities!* I did not escape such assumption even when I was on shipboard. I remember with especial vividness a Dutch captain, with whom I sailed over the Indian Ocean, and who liked to invite selected groups of passengers to break their fasts on hams and cheeses with him at dawn—and then settle down to a bout of bridge played "according to the rules of the Knickerbocker Club of New York," as he rather stiffly informed one guest who inquired whether he preferred any special set of conventions.) The colder the climate, the more inclement the weather, the worse the local hotels, the scarcer the domestic help, the greater the inability of women, singly or in groups, to put an appetizing meal on the table themselves, the stronger this conviction apparently became. But it was at a mammoth function, preceding the morning session of a journalistic state meeting, at which I was supposed to be the star speaker, that I finally decided there were to be no more breakfasts in my life.

The function in question was held at the hotel where I was staying, so at least I did not have to go out into a snowstorm. But it took place so early that room service, which operated intermittently at best, had not yet begun; therefore, I was not able to get a cup of (what passed for) coffee in that region before descending to the state apartments where large numbers of energetic lady journalists were bustling about. (Women in large numbers are terrifying to me per se. I like them very much individually, but something seems to make them more formidable when they are encountered collectively.) Some especially prominent guests were quite late in arriving, so it was more than an hour after the announced time for breakfast that we finally filed in to the dining room and sat down at a flower-decked table. In front of each place fruit cup, adorned with green leaves and liberally flavored with grenadine syrup, was awash in the melting ice which surrounded it. This sickening concoction was removed to make way for filet mignon with a rich mushroom sauce which had reached the tepid stage, French fried potatoes and stuffed tomatoes. Nothing even remotely resembling coffee had so far been offered. My hostess turned to me and looked at my untouched plate with concern.

"I'm afraid you're not enjoying your breakfast," she said kindly.

I have always been a very poor liar, but I did my best to assure her that the filet mignon looked delicious. "You see it isn't quite what I usually eat early in the morning though," I ended lamely. Her expression of concern deepened into one of real distress.

"We should have remembered how much of your life has been spent in New England!" she exclaimed. "Of course, you want your pie!"

Luncheons were not eliminated from my schedule quite as early in my career as breakfasts. For a long while I tried to include in my program those which might very well be important to me professionally and those which I knew would be delightful socially. But the result was that every time I made an exception to my "No Luncheon" rule, someone for whom I had not done this was offended and no doubt rightly so. Therefore, it seemed fairer and wiser to make no exceptions. Moreover, the statement, "Why, you have to eat somewhere!"—which is certainly true— ceased to carry weight. When you analyze the facts, you realize that (1) it does not take anywhere nearly as long to eat at home, alone, or with only some member of your family or of your secretarial staff at table with you, as it does if you eat at a club or a hotel or even in some private house where you cannot control or direct the service, with anywhere from six to six hundred persons in the same group; (2) you do not have to change your clothes if

88

you are eating at home, which you must do if you are going to a party; (3) you do not have to use up anywhere from fifteen to fifty minutes in getting to and from your destination; and (4) you do not have to wait indefinitely for the one guest who is lost, strayed or stolen when everyone else, including yourself and the cook, is impatient to begin the meal.

I cannot truthfully say that I have usually found the menus at ladies' luncheons either imaginative or intriguing; but they are at least one notch above breakfast menus; and if pleasantly stimulated beforehand by my *"café au lait au lit"* I can face, with a certain composure, the lukewarm chicken à la king, the wilted pear salad and the little mounds of "boughten" ice cream of which they not infrequently consist. Even the sweet sherry which precedes the more sophisticated luncheons, and the weak, fruit-laden old-fashioneds which precede the friskier ones, may be sipped and set aside without visible anguish. The same is true of the so-called coffee, which usually makes its appearance before the chicken, at the time when you might expect —if you had not learned better—a cup of hot clear soup. But the lost time is something else again.

I once consented, under pressure, to go, as an allegedly V. I. P., among a chosen group of alleged equal importance all the way from Crowley to New Orleans to attend a luncheon in honor of a very, very important person, who was passing through the city—only to find, after my arrival at the latter point, that the luncheon had been postponed for a week. As I was committed to work in Crowley for the next few days, I motored back there again and returned to New Orleans on the second date set. We had all been charged to arrive promptly at twelve o'clock, as the very, very important person was sailing for South America at four. But the sailing schedule was set back, so she strolled in unconcernedly at one-thirty. When I did a little angry addition, later on, I found that I had motored nearly eight hundred miles and wasted five days in order to attend a party which—once it got under way—lasted about an hour and a half. That was when I decided that luncheons, like breakfasts, would have to go by the board, if I were to get any work done and maintain at least the semblance of serenity.

As the day advances, the damage done to a working schedule by a social function becomes less and less grave, as I have observed before. But the main purpose of any such function is presumably to furnish relaxation and enjoyment; and personally I have not been able to find these at the average cocktail party. The different members of a small group of congenial spirits, seated in easy chairs around an open fire, on a restful verandah, or in an agreeable garden, can do a great deal to contribute to each other's pleasure, whether tea, coffee, orangeade or some stronger beverage is the refreshment provided by the host and hostess. A pitcher of milk or a bottle of beer, shared with even one such congenial spirit at bedtime, can bring a working day to a contented and tranquil close. But this is not the sort of entertainment that most persons have in mind when they suggest either a cocktail party or a night-cap. At least fifty people are generally squeezed into a room which would, perhaps, hold a dozen comfortably. There is no space for anyone to sit down. There is not the slightest chance of holding an intelligent conversation on any subject; and someone—usually more than one person —has not one or two cocktails or highballs, but a great many, and is correspondingly obnoxious.

I know that, theoretically, many affairs of state are set-tled at Washington cocktail parties; but I have always had grave doubts as to the reliability of this assumption. In fact, I am far more inclined to believe the story of the out-standing personage who had long submitted to such ordeals, because he had been assured it was necessary for the advancement of his career and the interests of the peo-ple he represented; and who finally made a bet that he could say the same thing to every person who stopped him long enough for an exchange of two sentences—and that not one of these persons would pay enough attention to know what he was saying. I cannot record his remark, because it is unprintable. But I can vouch for the fact that he won his bet.

Besides going to parties, a best-selling author is, of course, expected to give them. Among my other serious mistakes was the one I made when I assumed, after my husband's death, and my consequent withdrawal from official life, that I would be able to take the initiative in deciding whom I would invite to my house, when, how and why, and that I might even go for long periods without inviting anyone, if the state of my health or the pressure of my work indicated such seclusion. But it is very seldom that a day passes—never, I may say, without fear of exaggeration, that a week does so—when the telephone does not announce the arrival in town of a friend of a friend, of a faithful reader, of an energetic editor, or of some other visitor with an equally sound cause for consideration. (And that these causes *are* sound, I should be the last to deny.) Then comes the slight pause which indicates unmistakably that an invitation is in order, and that it should include not only the speaker, but certain other persons whom it is desirable or important that he should meet. Under normal circumstances—that is to say, unless I am already trying so desperately to meet a deadline that there are not enough minutes in the twenty-four hours to do so —I can easily manage a dinner of ten or twelve once a week and a mint julep party for about the same number one other evening within the same period—smaller groups or isolated guests more frequently, if they are willing to come no earlier than seven. And I greatly enjoy doing so. I take pride in my housekeeping. I like to use my best linen and china frequently and to prove what the combined efforts of Miss Clara and myself can produce in the way of good food, good drink and a generally agreeable atmosphere. I derive inspiration as well as pleasure from the guests who give me the privilege of their company—as long as there are not too many of them in the same group and as long as the groups do not come too close together. That is where the difficulty comes and it comes fairly often.

By way of example: I recently received, at the request of a prominent ecclesiastic, a delegation of five hundred persons who were attending a very important religious convention. I was delighted to do so. I have always considered my writing part of my Catholic action and, besides hoping that I could give the delegates pleasure, I felt it was an honor to have them in my house. We decorated this and the patio simply and the refreshments we served were very simple too. All in all, this reception was not much of a tax on my strength and, though it did keep me all day from my desk—it took place in the early afternoon—I felt I could and should make up for lost time. But this was on a Friday; and all the next day, other delegates who had not been able to come then, rang the doorbell with the trustful assumption that Saturday would do just as well. The following Monday I received three hundred members of a society to which I belong. This also, I was delighted to do. It is an organization designed to further better international relations, which is one of my chief interests and which has furnished the subject matter for much that I have written. A slightly more elaborate form of entertainment seemed indicated this time. The house was decorated anew, the decorations in the patio were freshened and enlarged, and we served punch, orange wine, coffee, sandwiches and cake. A beautiful young lady, dressed in a white, hoop-skirted dress, played old-fashioned airs on the square piano in the Victorian Room at the left of the front door; and on the gallery of the slave quarters at the rear of the patio a Cajun orchestra of five gave a delightful rendition of folk songs.

Naturally it took longer to prepare for this party and to recover from it than from the first. But two evenings later, my patio was opened to the public as part of a civic celebration in which I felt it was fitting that I should collaborate. By actual count of the guard who took the tickets at the door, thirteen hundred and fifty persons were present in my courtyard that night; and though I did my best to greet every one individually, it was a physical impossibility to circulate for three hours without brief periods of rest. Every time I left the patio, there were murmurs of resentment; these people said they had come to "meet the author" and, if they did not do so, they felt they had been defrauded.

The gentle reader may be forgiven for asking why I am not a better manager; that is to say, why I did not arrange matters so that these three functions should be spaced farther apart. The answer is easy: the preceding weeks and the following weeks were no less crowded.

XI

Although, as I have candidly confessed, functions such as those I have attempted to describe are, inevitably, fatiguing, both physically and mentally, and cut into the hours which should be set aside for creative writing, in order to achieve the best results, they nevertheless form a logical and normal part of a best-selling author's activities. I recognize them as such and appreciate the compliment they represent. But the constant invasion of privacy from sources which have no logical call upon me and which represent curiosity rather than admiration, is another phase of authorship which I have found it hard to endure. Apparently no writer is credited with having natural reserve, and a natural desire to enjoy the company of his family and friends as a human being and not as some kind of an exhibit.

I have already spoken of the difficulties which beset me in the course of my travels, as far as total strangers are concerned; these difficulties do not cease when I am at home. My New Orleans residence is a very lovely old house, once the home of General Beauregard, and now the property of a historical association. I selected it as a writing center during the winter months, partly because two bouts with bronchial pneumonia had unmistakably indicated the wisdom of seeking a mild climate and partly because its beauty was a source of delight to me. The room I chose for my study, at the left of the front door, is much lighter and airier than those farther to the rear, and therefore much better suited for my purposes. But I have had to practically abandon its use. The drivers

of ancient hacks beloved by tourists and the guides on the sight-seeing busses all proclaim my presence, and anyone mounting the exterior stairway could verify the statement by seeing me at my desk; these passers-by feel perfectly free to stop on the gallery and invite themselves in. "We have enjoyed your books so much, we wanted to see just how you *live*," a couple of breathless tourists frequently informed me. "Wouldn't you let us have just a teensy-weensy look around?" . . . "I am the librarian at East Podunk," another would say. "Is this really where you write your books? I promised I wouldn't go back home without finding out."

Eventually, I gave up the struggle and retreated to the slave quarters at the rear of the patio. These are invisible from the street and I have deliberately refrained from installing either a doorbell or a telephone. When I can find refuge there, I am reasonably safe from intrusion, but, as I have indicated before, I cannot do this if my work takes me to the opposite side of the globe, or hither and yon in search of source material, or, in any case, until the household machinery is running smoothly and the mail surmounted and arrangements made for the entertainment of visiting firemen who are passing through the city.

Once cloistered, however, I can sit down at a big desk and put out my tools and begin to work. I still use a pencil and the same kind of ruled copybook that I did when I was a child, scribbling on the right-hand page and keeping the left-hand page free for corrections and interpolations. It is a slow way to work, but it is a quiet one, and it has many advantages, as far as I am concerned, besides the obvious one that I am accustomed to it. At one stage of my progress, as I have said, I did my own typing, copying from my penciled draft and revising as I went along; I had to give up this method because I was too lame to sit at a typewriter, and I would not go back to it if I could. I have found that by reading aloud from my penciled script, I can catch the tedious repetition of words, phrases and ideas as I never could in any other way. The conversation that drags, the character that fails to develop, the situation which is forced or strained—these are all mercilessly revealed. And Deanie, to whom every word, every punctuation mark even, is read, does not spare her comments. If it is a true saying that no man is a hero to his valet, it is an even truer one that no author is an object of awe to his secretary, and fortunately so, for her carping criticism may save him from many a blunder. "You said yesterday that man had blue eyes," Deanie tells me caustically. "Now you have made them brown. Which do you really want?" . . . "Nobody says Wop around here; they say Dago, so I am putting Dago." . . . "Well, maybe you like that girl, the way you describe her, but I think she's a whited sepulchre, myself."

Hour after hour, day after day, the work of drafting, reading aloud, redrafting and redictating goes on. An old friend who is passing through the city drops in, unexpectedly, to call; Miss Clara, acting on instructions, tells her I am not at home. Though that is true enough, because I am in the slave quarters, not the big house, I am sorry to have missed seeing this old friend; it would have been pleasant to have talked with her for an hour about our school days in Boston, which seem so far away in every sense, and to find out what she is doing now. But there is that deadline. . . . Another friend, a more recent one, but still very dear to me, dies; I send flowers, which Deanie orders for me, but I do not go to the funeral, I do not even write a personal note till long afterward. (I write to my eldest son, hurried business letters, because he is also my lawyer; but weeks, even months go by when I do not write to his brothers, who are equally dear to me. Such letters would be merely personal, and I have no time for personal letters.) There is that deadline . . . I receive a gracious invitation to spend a week end in the country; I tell Deanie to decline it for me, with regrets. And the regrets are very real. The azaleas are at the height of their bloom just now, it would be very beautiful in the country; and there would be turtle soup and chicken parlow and spoon bread for dinner; there would be great good fellowship and I would come back to my work relaxed and refreshed. But there is that deadline. . . . The weather is growing warm and I have on a thick dress. I should put dresses like this one away for the summer and get my prints and muslins out of the bags in which they have been incased since last fall. But such dresses, which looked all right when they were put away, have a strange habit of shrinking during the winter and of unexpectedly revealing worn places; they are always either too long or too short as a result of changing fashions; they stick out in front or the waist puckers in the back as a result of a changing figure. Deanie is very critical of such defects. Even on the rare occasions when I put on something which gives me the (very temporary) feeling of being a glass of fashion and a mold of form, she finds some flaw in it. I had better leave those poor old thin dresses where they are until the book is done, even though I nearly perish with the heat meanwhile. For Deanie will let me have no peace until I have given them away to worthy causes and gone out to buy new ones. And I have no time to bother with clothes just now. There is that deadline. . . . I have a little nagging pain in my left side. It is not bad enough to really hamper me in my work, but

102

I am unpleasantly conscious of it; I wish it would go away. Also, I cannot help remembering that the last time I had a physical checkup, the diagnostician, after a thorough and very painful series of tests, told me that the little nagging pain—which he called by a long Latin name—signified a condition which might become serious and that it should be carefully watched. It is a long while since that last checkup, as he has several times reminded me, and I ought to have another. But there is that deadline. . . . I would like to go and get my hair washed, for I need a shampoo badly. That does not take all day, leaving me spent and sore, like a physical checkup; it takes only an hour or so, under the skillful ministrations of Coralie, my Creole hairdresser. But it constitutes an interruption, and an interrupted train of thought is as hard to piece together again as a length of lace that has been torn into fragments. I would not lose an hour if I went to Coralie's house; I would lose at least three or four. So I had better wash my hair myself, at two in the morning, as I did last week—the words were blurring by then, so I could not write any more and I did not lose any time from the book. And there is that deadline. . . . I hear church bells ringing and I would like to throw down my pencil and close my copy book and go to Benediction. Churchgoing has always been a joyous and rewarding part of my religion and frequent,

103

almost daily, attendance at some rite was once a habit with me. Now I go only to those which are a requirement of the Catholic church—to Mass on Sundays and other Holy Days of Obligation, to Confession and to Communion once a year. I miss that attendance at Benediction which was so spontaneous; it is a service of which I am extremely fond and it always left me with a special sense of serenity. But there is that deadline. . . .

I wish that source material did not present such a problem. When I am dealing with present-day events and conditions, or those within the ready memory of living persons, such material is not overhard to cope with, given time enough to do so. But when I am delving into the past, a search must be made through old periodicals, old letters and old histories, and sometimes the tales they tell are contradictory. Then it is necessary to search still further for documentation that will corroborate either one version or another or, if that is missing, to take the responsibility of choosing between the two, as I have to do—for instance—regarding the length of General Beauregard's sojourn in the house which is now my winter residence and which bears his name. (Some authorities, whom I respect, insist that he lived there only briefly, as a lodger, after the War Between the States. Others, whom I also respect, insist that this sad story was the anticlimax to a very happy one, when, after years of widowerhood, he brought his second wife, Caroline Deslonde, there as a bride, and that it was there they had a happy honeymoon.) Sometimes, on the other hand, only one account of some distant but dramatic event still survives; in that case, looking for it is like hunting for a needle in a haystack. But the search must be made, if the incident in question has story value.

In the early days of my work on *Crescent Carnival,* I heard, quite by chance, that once in the course of the French Opera Company's annual visits to New Orleans, when the singers were arriving by boat, some of the city fathers went down the Mississippi River, in a tug, to meet them, and that a gala supper was served aboard ship, to the accompaniment of both song and speeches. I immediately visualized this episode as providing an effective scene for my novel; but though I could find plenty of persons who were sure it had taken place, and a few who had a vague recollection that some member of their family had been there when it did, of course I could not present an event as factual on such slender evidence. Moreover, these same persons assured me that the company had generally come to New Orleans by train, after disembarking at New York, rather than direct from France, especially during the latter part of the troupe's existence; that the occasion in which I was interested must have been an isolated one; and that since the visits of the opera company covered approximately a fifty-year period, it would be virtually impossible to discover when the one which interested me took place.

I long ago adopted Napoleon's slogan, "If it is possible, it can be done; if it is impossible, it must be done"; and, in this instance, for a wonder, I was not especially short of time—or rather, I did not realize that I was, for the book was hardly under way, and I did not yet visualize the impending pressure to get it done. I went to the offices of the *Times-Picayune,* and asked for permission to examine its files, beginning with the year when the French Opera Company had inaugurated its visits. Permission was pleasantly accorded, and huge, bound volumes of yellow, brittle newspapers were taken from their shelves and laid out in sequence on a large table. I knew I did not have to inspect every separate entry, because the opera company always arrived in the autumn; but I began with those daily papers issued in October and searched straight along until I came to those issued in December. After a week in which I did nothing else, I experienced the glorious sensation of victory: I discovered that in 1887 the French Opera Company, headed by Mlle. de Rinkly had come over from

France on the *Nantes* and that Mr. Frederick Mauge went down to the river to meet them!

The scene which I wrote as a result of this discovery produced the desired effect; but, as I have said, I could not have ferreted it out if I had been short of time. On another occasion, I had to find a different way of getting around the time element.

Mrs. Fernand Claiborne, née Marie Louise Villeré, whose girlhood reminiscences formed the nucleus for my story, *Once on Esplanade,* told me about a horse race which had made a deep impression, and with reason, on her youthful mind. This much she could tell me: her beloved brother, Omer, had ridden in a race for gentlemen jockeys, and he had promised that, if he won, he would give her the silver spurs which were offered as a prize. When well out in front of the other contestants, one of Omer's stirrups broke—and then the other. As he crossed the finish line, the saddle turned, and he fell with his horse on top of him. When he tried to rise, he found he could not stand; he had broken an ankle. The rider who had come in second, obviously a very poor sport, called out triumphantly, "You'll never get to the scales to be weighed in. You lose to me!" But Omer was not one to have his victory snatched from him so ingloriously; despite his broken ankle, he managed to reach the scales, was weighed in, declared the winner, and presented with the spurs, which he duly bestowed upon his little sister!

When Mrs. Claiborne told me this story, she confessed that she could not remember exactly where or when the race had occurred or who, besides her brother, had ridden in it. I was already so close to my deadline that it was unthinkable I should take a week, or even a day off to pore over old newspapers. But I was determined to use the episode, for I not only saw story material in it; I thought I also saw movie material. (No one else has yet done so, but that is beyond the point. I still believe someone will, eventually!) However, I could not possibly print it, unless I could authenticate it in every detail; no fictitious names had been used in *Once on Esplanade*, and I could not present a man as a champion unless he deserved this honor, much less could I run the risk of libel by attributing poor sportsmanship to another, without being ready to back up my charge, should occasion arise. I appealed, through the most influential channels at my command, to sportsmen and sports writers both aging and youthful; all of them assured me that they had never heard of such a race and one of my (hitherto) most reliable advisers told me flatly that it had never taken place—that Mrs. Claiborne's memory must be playing her the tricks which are not uncommon in the case of elderly ladies.

Still convinced that my heroine knew what she was talking about, and still undaunted, though by this time I felt as though I were running a race myself—I was now within a few days of my deadline—I tried one last expedient: I inserted a lengthy advertisement in the New Orleans papers, offering a reward of one hundred dollars for authentic information regarding a horse race won by the late Omer Villeré, in spite of broken stirrups and a broken ankle, and over the protests of his runner-up. Within twenty-four hours I had the evidence I wanted, and the discoverer of the buried item, Marie Louise Clark, has been one of my most valuable assistants ever since. But even Mrs. Clark, well-nigh infallible as she is when it comes to research, cannot always do successful delving within the space of twenty-four hours; and the publisher who is clamoring for his story would be the first to complain—and rightly so—if material which would not stand up under rigid examination were incorporated in the text for which the author is responsible.

So, all in all, there are no Saturday afternoons off, for either Deanie or myself, no Sunday afternoons, either, for me. Sundays are the days when I must forge forward with the pencil script for, with everyone else bent on relaxation or enjoyment, I can be surer then of freedom from interruption than at any other time. So, after we come back

109

from Mass at St. Mary's Italian Church across the way, Deanie disappears to parts unknown and I eat my solitary dinner and go back to the slave quarters. And long, long afterward, Miss Clara calls to me from the rear gallery, "I know you don't want to be interrupted, but have you any idea what time it is?"

I have not the slightest idea what time it is in New Orleans, for I have been in another world and the time in that world is the only one of which I am conscious. I have begun to live with a group of people whom I never knew before, but whom I am, at last, getting to know very well. I have to. If they were not real to me, they would never be real to anyone else. I only hope they will not make me too much trouble, that they will behave as it is reasonable for them to behave and as I want them to behave. But I cannot be sure of it. The first thing I know, Anne will be refusing to marry John and Edward will fall down and break his leg and Aunt Nellie will leave her money, which Mary needs so desperately, to an orphan asylum. Well, I should not complain, if only I do not have to deal with another cat like Pinkham.

I shall never forget Pinkham, who complicated my existence in such an unexpected way and to such a very great degree when I was writing *Also the Hills*. The house on Farman Hill, which provided the setting for the major part of that story, had its prototype in reality, like most of the houses I have used for settings; and my friends, Daniel and Sadie Carr, the owners of the real house, were most kind about helping me with my local color. When the book was about two-thirds done, I realized that I had said nothing about any birds on Farman Hill, and I was sure there must be some; so I wrote to Mrs. Carr, asking for authentic information. By return mail, she sent me a long, detailed letter, which ended, ". . . and I think the reason we have always been fortunate in having so many birds about the place is because our cat, Pinkham, has never molested them. He does not take the least interest in birds."

Forgetting all about the rest of the letter, I sat staring in horror at those last sentences. Of course a house like Farman Hill would have had a cat like Pinkham in it. And there was no cat in my story. I tried to tell myself that no one else would notice the omission, that even Mrs. Carr herself had not suggested the addition of Pinkham to the cast of characters. But my arguments were unconvincing to me. Finally I went to bed, and every time I turned over, facing the fireplace, I seemed to see the eyes of a reproachful cat glaring at me from the spot where the andirons customarily stood. At four o'clock in the morning I could bear it no longer. I got up, flung on my clothes and went to my desk. Then I took the script of *Also the Hills* from

111

its box and, beginning with chapter one, introduced Pinkham in all the places where I knew he belonged!

After that, I was at peace again. But such interpolations entail very considerable revision when the script in question has already reached its third, and presumably its final stage, as it had in that case. The second stage—the result of reading aloud from the penciled draft—is represented by a typescript done in triple spacing, which allows for further revisions, corrections and additions. There are usually a good many of these, so many that numerous pages are typed over and over again, still in triple space. But when we get around to double spacing, we think our script is ready to send off to our publisher, who, long before this, had been hounding us for it through the expressive media of air mail, telegrams and long-distance calls. The appearance of another character at this point would mean that the third draft would also have to be done over again. What is more, it means that something would have to be done to placate both Deanie and the publisher. . . .

Reflecting on all this, I call to Miss Clara that I will be up in a minute. But I do not go up in a minute. I read through what I have written that afternoon and it seems to me very, very bad. I know it will seem even worse the next day, when I read it aloud to Deanie; she will question my spelling and correct my slang and tell me that my

112

hero's type of love-making went out with hoop skirts. Well, it cannot be helped. But I have an uneasy feeling about our pawnbroker. I do not know very much about pawnbrokers. How do they talk? Where do they live? Would a pawnbroker be likely to have several children, and if he did, would some of them help him in his shop? Or would his devoted wife do that? It is too bad that I did not stick to politicians. I am more familiar with their habits than those of pawnbrokers.

The pawnbroker does not represent my only source of worry; over and over again, all day long, I have been eluded by the *mot juste* that I have been seeking. Perhaps if I make one more search through Webster's Unabridged and Roget's Thesaurus. . . . And I had better get out that folder where I file away names. There are several Leonardos in my fiction already; someone will be writing in to remind me of this and anyway, I am disappointed with the repetition myself. Leopoldo is almost the same. Emelio sounds effeminate. Alphonso is a cliché. Wait a minute—what about Ambrosio? Yes, I think Ambrosio might do; I will write it in everywhere that I have previously written Leonardo, because otherwise I will forget to make the revision some place and confusion will result. Then, tomorrow morning, when I start reading to Deanie, I will see how Ambrosio sounds. . . .

I put out the lights and close the door of the study. It is very quiet in the patio, so quiet that it is hard to believe that this is in the heart of a great city. The fountain makes a little trickling sound and the breeze stirs the camellia bushes, ever so slightly. There are stars overhead and the air is soft and mild. It would be pleasant to sit in the patio for a little while. But it must be very late now, and suddenly I know that I am terribly tired, so tired that I would rather go to bed than sit anywhere, so tired that I can hardly drag myself up the steps of the back gallery, so tired that I do not want any supper. (But of course it is long past suppertime anyway.) At the head of the stairway Miss Clara is waiting for me accusingly.

"You promised me, when you wrote that last novel, you'd never work this way again," she says. "And you're just as bad as ever. I don't see what you get out of it. . . . Mrs. Crager brought fifty more books to be autographed for the Basement Book Shop. She said she'd send for them the first thing in the morning. Just the same, I hope you won't touch them tonight. And, for heaven's sake, let me fix you a drink and get you a sandwich. You can't go to bed without anything in your stomach. The first thing I know, you'll be sick again."

XII

Of course Miss Clara is not the only person who has wondered what I get out of it, though since she has been watching me in action for twenty years now, she comments on the general situation with more feeling than most. And very often I have asked myself the same question. As I have confessed, there was one time when I was so nearly sure the game was not worth the candle that I was tempted to give it up. But now I know I shall go on playing it, as well as I can, to the end.

There are several reasons for this. It is normal for anyone who has been independent for a long time to cherish such independence. If I were not a writer I should have to turn to my sons for at least partial support and this would be very hard for me. It would also be hard for them and their wives and their children, not only financially but in many other ways. They have a right to their own mode of life and their own viewpoint, unhampered by the mode of life and the viewpoint of a previous generation. And I have a right to mine. So far our relations have always been happy and harmonious. I want very much to keep them so. I do not believe I could if my associations with my family were based on necessity rather than on inclination.

It is fair to say, in connection with the terms "self-support" and "mode of life," that I do not refer to bare necessities. I could, without being dependent on my sons, still be sure of simple food, simple shelter and simple clothing, even if I did little or no writing. But I would have to prepare the food myself, I would have to do my own sewing and my own housework. Because of my spinal handicap, this would be very hard for me and it would also show very poor judgment; no woman with a proper sense of balance should renounce the type of work for which she is fitted, in every way, in order to do a type of work for which she is far less fitted.

Carrying candor a little further, it is fair to state that I know my frame of mind would be far less contented than it is now if I had only the bare necessities of life; I would rather work hard and have enough money for certain diversions and luxuries, than to be idle and forfeit those which give me great pleasure. I do not have much time off, but I can crowd an immense amount of enjoyment into such leisure as I do have. For instance, when I go to New York for editorial conferences, these keep me busy nearly every day and a good many evenings. But meanwhile I can stay at a comfortable hotel. When I can steal an hour or so to myself out of working hours, I can shop wherever I choose—and, under those conditions, a great many useful and beautiful things can be bought in a very short time. The evenings when I am not working I can go, in a comfortable, hired car, to a restaurant where I eat an excellent meal at my ease and afterward, to a theater where, ensconced in an excellent seat, I can see an amusing or inspiring play—and theatergoing is my favorite form of entertainment. I can do all this without worrying about the cost. I should be very sorry to forego such brief interludes of relaxation and stimulation and I should be sorrier still if I could not afford to invite the various members of my family and my staff, and occasionally my friends, to share them with me. I should be sorriest of all to feel that I had to forego the pleasure of providing my grandchildren with some of the "advantages" and "treats" which their parents' more limited budgets will not permit. All this seems to me entirely normal for a matriarch.

It is also normal for anyone to derive a certain amount of satisfaction from success along a chosen line, especially if that success has been hard won. A cessation of work would, inevitably, mean a cessation of such satisfaction; moreover, complete idleness would be as wearisome as constant over-endeavor. Of course, if it were possible to find the happy medium between the two, that would be ideal; but so far it has not been possible. Each new undertaking brings with it unexpected ramifications involving more study, more research, more correspondence, more conferences, more travel. And if I must choose between the horns of a dilemma, my choice is to go ahead at full speed rather than to come to a full stop. There is always a thrill and a challenge in a race toward a distant goal.

There is another kind of satisfaction too, of even more consequence than the material one. This is the satisfaction derived from the feeling that your work has given pleasure or encouragement or help, or even all three, to other people. I have spoken earlier of the disagreeable and depressing letters that come in and the ones that make unreasonable demands; but I would not be fair if I did not speak of the far greater number of appreciative letters, the letters that do far more for me than I can hope to do for their writers. Every mail brings at least one of these, usually several; they were especially numerous and especially significant during World War II. "I read all night from *Fielding's Folly* to my fellow refugees in a bomb shelter and we forgot we were in danger." . . . "I have been in the hospital six weeks now and most of the other men have been here longer. We have some of your books in the ward and we take turns in reading them and we then talk them over. It does help to pass the time. We thought perhaps you would like to know." . . . "I am a Wren, but I have been invalided home with tuberculosis and told that I can probably never go back to active duty. I lie all day in the

118

garden, reading. I am reading all your books that I can get hold of. Here is a list of the ones in our local library. If it would not be too much trouble, perhaps you would let me know whether I could get the others and, if so, where. I have been told that some of them are out of print." Some of them were temporarily out of print, in England, during the war, because of the paper shortage, though they have now all been reissued. In the course of this period, I received a clipping from a London newspaper, unaccompanied by any personal word:

Wanted, a copy of *The Great Tradition* for a young girl who is dying and whose parents have not been able to procure a copy for her. Any reasonable price gladly paid. Address XYZ [etc.].

Letters written during the stress and strain of war are by no means the only ones that are a source of encouragement to an author; the ones which are written with no other purpose than to say thank you give as much pleasure to their recipients as the books which inspired them can possibly have given to their readers. These letters come in by the dozen and sometimes they are very moving.

"I have spent so many happy hours with your books that I have felt for some time I would like to write you and express my sincere thanks for all the pleasure you have given me," one such letter tells me.

"I am a busy housewife and mother of three lovely children, but oh, how restricted life can be at times! I cope with housework, baking, mending, the children, and at the same time I do try to be a happy companion to my husband. But you know it can be awfully difficult to be an interesting and inspiring wife when for days and weeks on end life holds nothing but the daily round, the common task.

"Your books have opened up many beautiful and fascinating vistas for me. In your company I have seen many strange and lovely cities and have learned of many different customs and ways of living. All this has been a great delight to me, but you have helped me in a more important way still. Your deep conviction that the role of wife and mother is the most worthwhile a woman can have, has done more to help me over the drab, dull spots than anything else I can think of. Your lovely heroines have inspired me to buck up and try again when I am in danger of degenerating into a mere overworked housekeeper. Once more I become a real personality with a real interest in life, and, I hope, a more stimulating wife and mother in consequence.

"Thank you for all the happiness you have given me,

and I hope this letter may have given you some small pleasure, too."

Very different, but possibly even more poignant, is a letter which comes from French Guinea. Something of its spirit is lost in translation, but most of this is indestructible: "I cannot resist the desire of expressing my admiration for your *Honor Bright*. Since 1945 I have read many American novels containing detailed descriptions of your charming South; but none has touched me as much as yours. You may ask why. Perhaps because I read it at a time when many illusions had been lost, perhaps because on the hard roads where I work (I am a truck driver in French Occidental Africa) the feeling of delightful freshness in *Honor Bright* was doubly vivid under a hot sun and after a great effort.

"Anyway, the forty-year-old man who drives a five-ton truck on the road from Soudan to the Ivory Coast has been touched over and over again by the pure beauty that comes from your novel. You see, madame, here in Africa, we lack beauty and ideals, cleanliness and faith. Everything is exaggerated. The work, the sun, the drinking, what passes for love. It is inexpressibly comforting to sit down after work and open your book; to think that, under different circumstances, we could have been like Jerry, that we could have met and loved Honor or some other sweet southern lady. Then we can dream a little and during those few hours something precious has been added to the time which Destiny gives us.

"It is very sad, madame, that so many of my compatriots see in your people only chewers of gum or the G. I. in our Parisian bars. Why is the wonderful South, with names so reminiscent of our old France, so unknown there?

"Perhaps you are wondering why I am writing to you. That too is very simple and very clear.

"First of all, because I think that when someone has done you good, even indirectly, even without knowing it, one should say thank you. Therefore, though I am convinced this letter may never reach you, I feel obligated to say just that. Thank you for having made me forget the jungle, the fallen down bridges, the impassable roads, the indolent natives. Thank you for having helped me to remember that somewhere in the world beauty, loyalty and faith still survive, that there are not only oil, gas, machines, regimentation and freight to carry around—for whom and what for? Secondly, it is because I would like Frances Parkinson Keyes, if she ever receives this letter, to send me something from her, something characteristic of the South. Not a photograph or an autograph. I am not a collector. But I want something which will give me proof

122

that she exists and that the Virginia of which she writes exists also."

Communications such as these are, inevitably, very moving; they act as a spur to greater and greater endeavor. When a tribute is paid in person, this is more moving still. Two years ago, on the eve of a fashionable wedding in New Orleans, I received a telephone call, asking me if I would attend the wedding. The bride's aunt, whom I scarcely knew, was speaking. She hoped I understood, she said, why I had not been invited in the first place; the wedding was really a family affair. I told her that I understood perfectly, that I had never expected to be invited; I might truthfully have added that I had not realized such a function was impending, but I was afraid this might hurt her feelings, so I waited for her to go on. It then appeared that the groom's mother had come from New England, that she had wanted very much to meet me and had been disappointed because she had not. The bride's relatives were naturally eager to do everything possible for the pleasure of this lady, a stranger in their midst. So if I would waive ceremony. . . .

It was extremely inconvenient for me to take time out to go to a noon wedding, but something impelled me to do so. As I went down the receiving line and was presented to the groom's mother, she grasped my hand and asked me to come back again, when she could speak to me quietly. I waited until the line had thinned and then I did as she asked. This time I saw that her eyes were filled with tears.

"The son who was married today is my only child," she told me. "And he has been away from home, at school and college, for a long while. I have been a widow a great many years. My sister has been my one constant companion. Now she has died too—a slow, lingering death from cancer. For the last two years the only release we could secure for her has come from your books. I was reading to her from one of them, a religious book, a few hours before she died. It helped us both at the very end. I had to tell you this. I had to thank you."

It so happened that this experience, which made a deep impression on me, occurred not long before another, which was no less moving, though in a different way. I had gone to Mérida, in Yucatán, which for years I had wanted to visit and where I thought a long-delayed vacation was at last ahead of me. I spent it in bed, as a result of having injured my eardrums by flying when I had a cold and, besides being in great pain, I was of course bitterly disappointed. On the last day of my stay in the city, I crawled into my clothes, took one of the funny little horse-drawn cabs which still offer the current means of transportation,

124

and drove around for an hour. My attention was arrested by a display of gold filigree jewelry in a shopwindow, so I asked the driver to stop and got out to look at it. Next door to the jewelry store was a bookstore and I turned, instinctively, from one to the other. Almost the entire display in the window of the bookstore consisted of *El Camino del Rio—The River Road* in Spanish.

I stared at it in stupefaction for a moment and then I went inside and introduced myself to the proprietor. He received me with enthusiasm. Yes, the book was going very well, he told me—perhaps better than any other of mine so far, though they all did well. The only trouble was, he had difficulty in getting enough to supply the demand. Was there any way I could help him to get a larger allotment? And when could he expect a new novel? He had heard there was going to be another, this time with the scene laid in France. . . .

I tried to listen to him and to answer him courteously and helpfully. But I was absorbed in watching the people who streamed by in the street and I was thinking very hard. Fully three-fourths of the women going by were wearing the straight-cut native dresses made of white cotton and embroidered in bands of bright color around the square neck, the elbow sleeves and the wide hems; they had black *rebozos* wound about their heads and throats and *alpar-*

gatas on their bare feet. The men's costumes were almost invariably loose white trousers and loose white jackets and many of them did not even wear sandals. They looked primitive and they looked poor. But evidently these people in Yucatán were buying my books, just as the people in Helsinki and the Canary Islands and Capetown and Manila were buying them—because they wanted them. Yes, and the people in Paris and The Hague and Stockholm and Madrid, in Washington, D.C. and Brattleboro, Vermont and Little Rock, Arkansas and New York City. And this meant that, whatever the critics said, I must somehow have succeeded in writing about the pleasures and sorrows, the desires and needs that are universal, in a way that could be universally understood and enjoyed. I was in touch with the human family throughout the world—rich and poor, old and young, wise and ignorant—because of my books; especially because of one book, which until then I had thought cost too much, both in cash and in kind. And suddenly I knew that no price was too high for such fellowship and such communion, that everything which had gone into my lifework was worth-while.